How to Make the World a Better Place

for WOMEN

In Five Minutes a Day

• • • • •

Donna Jackson

HYPERION

New York

Library of Congress Cataloging-in-Publication Data
Jackson, Donna.
   How to make the world a better place for women in five minutes a day
/ by Donna Jackson.—1st ed.
        p.   cm.
   Includes bibliographical references.
   ISBN 1-56282-907-6 : $6.95
      1. Feminism—United States—Miscellanea.   2. Social Action—United States—Miscellanea.   3. Sexism—United States—Prevention—Miscellanea.   4. Women's rights—United States—Miscellanea.
I. Title.
HQ1426.J28   1992   92-20739
305.42′0973—dc20   CIP

First Edition

10 9 8 7 6 5 4 3 2 1

Contents

Never underestimate the ability
of a small, dedicated group of
people to change the world; indeed
it's the only thing that ever
has changed the world.

—*Margaret Mead*

Acknowledgments

This book could not have been written without the help, support, and guidance of so many colleagues and friends. Foremost, I am indebted to my friend Sue Browder, who tirelessly shared her talents and generously lent her vision to this project. The consulting and research she contributed were integral to the creation of this book, and many of these pages are the result of what I feel can only be termed a collaborative effort.

I am forever grateful to my dear friend Stephanie von Hirschberg who dispensed daily pep talks and read each page of this manuscript with a careful, insightful eye; to Zenji Nakazawa for his love and friendship; to Mark Levine who generously shared his legal expertise; to Meg Siesfeld, Tom Hartman, and Kelly Good McGee for their cheering belief; to Julia Mayben for her fast and competent fact-checking skills; to Tracy Oliver, Victoria Secunda, Kay Cullen-Mogey, Catherine Johnson, Ann Bowie Rice, and Jan Esielonis for their enduring support and friendship.

My thanks, too, to my supportive family—my mother, Marcia Strok, often filled my refrigerator with food and set flowers on my desk as I met deadlines; my brothers, Jay and Chip; stepfather Michael Strok; and grandfather Elmer Martin Jackson, Jr., all cheered me on and offered much encouragement along the way. I'm especially thankful to my brother Don for his friendship and faith in me; to Kim Eshlemen for her sisterly kinship; as well as to Donna Larsen, Mary Waters Wetherhold, Annabell Harris, Janice Jackson, and Lois Lipsett for their familial warmth, friendship, and the examples they've set for me since I was a girl of what women can accomplish and stand for in this life.

I'm deeply grateful to my agent, Geri Thoma, for her instant belief in this project as well as for her guidance; to my editor Judith Riven at Hyperion for immediately getting behind this book, full force, and for recognizing the pressing need for its existence; to Bob Miller whose faith in this project right from the start kept us on a fast and even keel; to Vicki DiStasio who tirelessly made sense of fax pages and updates; as well as to all the others at Hyperion who helped to make this book happen so quickly, without ever losing their enthusiasm.

I am also lucky to have the understanding of my colleagues and friends at *New Woman,* namely Karen Walden and Susan Kane, who graciously understood my need to do this project even while it meant postponing a deadline or two, to Joanne Serling, who held down the fort while I finished these pages, and to former editors Pat Miller and Gay Bryant, both of whom gave me early faith in myself as a writer.

This book is dedicated to the memory of my father, Jay Jackson, who handed down to me the love of words, and who taught me through deed, word, and attitude that a woman is never less than a man.

Introduction

When you talk to the average woman these days, you hear a kind of fear and concern you haven't heard in decades—a concern that women actually have *not* come "a long way, baby," despite all the progress we've made. Events of the last year—ranging from the Senate's rough treatment of Anita Hill during the confirmation hearings of Judge Clarence Thomas to the slow but determined overturning of a woman's right to choose abortion as guaranteed in *Roe* v. *Wade* to the vetoing of every family and maternity leave law that's come up for vote to date (while all industrialized nations but ours and South Africa have firm family leave policies)—have a lot of women wondering if we're *ever* going to see a home sweet America in which women have true equality.

Recently, it seems every woman I speak with has suddenly "sat up" and realized that women's status in our society has not progressed in the way we thought it would have by now. As editor-at-large and a frequent TV and radio spokesperson for *New Woman* magazine and author of dozens of articles for national magazines, I spend a lot of time listening to and talking with women across the country. And in the past decade of working with women, I've never heard women—many of whom wouldn't strictly classify themselves as feminists or activists—as frustrated as they are right now.

In the wake of the Thomas hearings, one young woman I spoke with, who has always said feminism wasn't for her generation, said her friends (in their mid-twenties) suddenly "woke up after the Anita Hill hearings in a way we never had before; until now I guess we've pretty much always considered women's rights a done deal. But now we're all saying, 'Where will all this stop? Have we come as far as we thought?' " Another woman—a fifty-two-year-old communications director, wife, and mom—said sadly, "Throughout the Senate hearings, I felt an overwhelming sense of helplessness. Women's rights have already slid so far backwards it's unbelievable. Now that Thomas is on the Supreme Court, we can kiss *Roe* v. *Wade* goodbye. The worst part, though, is that when I look at issues like harassment, or abortion, or when I read frightening new studies like those showing that rape and date rape are rising dramatically, *I* feel absolutely powerless to make the situation any better, and so do all of my friends."

What we're seeing in the nineties is a revival of women's consciousness on a grand scale, a revival which has us perched on the edge of a new kind of women's movement—a "gentle" women's movement, if you will. But this new kind of awareness, which is awakening women all the way from Madison Avenue to Main Street U.S.A., isn't like the feminism of the past: while some of these women stand proudly under the "feminist label," many others say they don't want to be labeled as feminists. Who are they? These are ordinary women of all ages—the young mothers and grown-up daughters of the women's movement—all part of the American mainstream, all struggling to attain a female vision of the American dream. Some are homemakers who, even though they may have chosen not to work outside the home, believe that women deserve the same choices and options as men. Others are single, working moms struggling to make ends meet on salaries that don't begin to match men's. Others are successful, single working women who, seeing the overburdened lives of the women around them, wonder if they'll ever be able to juggle a marriage, family, and career. And many are married, working women, already well established in their careers, doing well financially, living full lives which include loving relationships with men and kids. Almost all assumed, until recently, that feminism had already protected their futures.

Yet all of these women, like you and me, find their sense of justice is offended more and more often these days. It's offended, for instance, when they read a news story which tells how a woman like forty-one-year-old Lucille Anne Riccitelli was recently required by a Providence, Rhode Island, judge to obtain her husband's written permission before the court would allow her to drop her husband's last name and use her maiden one (though no law existed requiring her to do so). Or when they see a magazine like *Esquire* run a cover story (June 1990) called "Your Wife: An Owner's Manual," with a pictorial showing a sketch of a sink's plumbing drawn over a woman's midsection, captioned: "Her plumbing: how much should you know?" Or when they turn on the TV and see a woman seductively walking across a beach in a bikini as the announcer for Coors Light beer says, "Coors Light. Because if you don't watch your figure, who *will?*"

These are ordinary women who, even though they may have "arrived" in their careers, see that something around them is still not fair, not quite right. As a result, they want to find a way in which they can make the world better not only for themselves but for all women (and, as a by-product, for the men they love). Yet they want to do this in their own *individual* way, and on their own personal schedule. Not as part of a uniform group.

Indeed, women's concern, energy, and desire for change do put us on the brink of a new, "gentle" women's movement—yet right now, our energy has nowhere to go. Our consciousness is all raised up with no avenue to take toward change. Said one woman I spoke with who is in her early thirties: "I bought the bestseller *Backlash* [by Susan Faludi]. And I read *The Beauty Myth* [by Naomi Wolf]. They were wonderful, but they only pointed to the problems women face today. What I'm wondering is, what are the *solutions?*" Other women have said that while they've been glad to be able to call the National Organization for Women and a host of other helpful women's organizations, they long to do something more than just send in a check. Yet another woman says, "I feel this great need to act . . . but what can one person do?" And another: "My days are so taken up with a job, children, and a husband, I barely have time to do anything else." Upset and aware as they are, they feel powerless to help make a difference. They feel they have little or no time in their hectic lives to harness their concern and anger and turn it into the kind of power that makes grand-scale change happen.

So, the pressing question is, Where to from here? We really do want to make the world better for ourselves, and for all women—including the generations to come. Yet where do we turn? Who has the time? What are the answers? Besides, how can one person make any *real* difference when it comes to the widespread, global concerns women face?

How to Make the World a Better Place for Women—in Five Minutes a Day empowers you, as an individual woman, to get up and *do something* about the ways in which our society limits a woman's life, by offering you a wealth of little known, simple ways *you* can make a difference. Here, personal activism is redefined; instead of needing to be part of a large organization in order to foster change, you can make critical change happen from right where you are (your home, your office, the grocery store, the day care center), during the course of an otherwise ordinary day.

There's no use in letting it overwhelm us when we take in all the headlines out there today, telling us how women's rights are being undermined. Sure, it's scary to witness the campaign to overturn *Roe* v. *Wade;* or the way a woman is treated if she complains about sexual harassment; or our leaders' vetoing of laws that would guarantee women family leave and help with child care; or to see that so many men still aren't picking up enough slack with the kids and the housework; or to see women's health concerns get put on a back burner to men's. But such news *needn't* drive us to despair; even the most overwhelming of problems we women face can be met head on, and solutions reached, if everyone takes just a little action, and gets just a little bit involved, every day.

No one, single-handedly, can keep the President from continuing to veto laws which would protect women's jobs if they take maternity leave. Alone, no woman among us can make sure that *Roe* v. *Wade* isn't overturned, or that we don't lose our "right to choose" on a state level, as well as on a federal one. And by ourselves, we can't keep sexist and demeaning images of women from creeping into television and print advertisements. But all of us *can* do a little bit, here and now, to make grand, sweeping change occur. If only we know how.

Now you do: here's a set of "This Insults Women" stickers so that the next time you see an offensive ad or poster (like the popular one showing a woman's naked belly branded with the words "U.S.D.A. Choice"), you can take this sticker and "stick it to it"; a poster stating the federal guidelines concerning sexual harassment—so you can post it over the water cooler at your workplace; a way to shop for products made by companies whose family-friendly policies make life easier for working moms; and a method to find headhunters who help women break through the glass ceiling.

Some "things you can do" address lighter issues, others are deadly serious. For instance, should you or anyone you know ever be the unfortunate victim of rape, you'll have the information you need to make sure you get to a hospital which has the new rape evidence-gathering kit, so you'll be sure the offender will be locked away (where he can't rape again).

From the personal to the political, it's all right here. Including your senator's voting record on abortion, and his office phone number, so you can let him know you won't vote for him this election year, if his vote doesn't protect *your* rights. And a postcard pre-addressed to the White House, printed with the words "Let The President Know," in case you want to let the President know how you feel about his stand on the issues which most concern women today.

Most of the ways you can make a difference covered here are unbelievably easy. They're the kinds of things you can do in a spare five or ten minutes a day, and would do, if only you had all the information about who to contact, and how to make an impact, already at your fingertips. Now you have that information *and* those contacts. Fast solutions are provided on a vast array of issues dear to women's hearts, so *you* can pick those issues you care most about, and start to make the changes you long for—personally, professionally, politically, globally. All you need is five minutes a day, because all the legwork has been done for you.

One note: While all the numbers and addresses compiled here were completely up to date when we went to press, offices do move and phone numbers do change. If you find that's the case when you contact the resources here, don't give up—simply take a few seconds to call information, get the new number, and then take action.

Knowledge *is* power, and *How to Make the World a Better Place for Women—in Five Minutes a Day* gives you a set of simple, effective "power tools" to rebuild and redesign the shape of things to come.

In the 1990s, women have a newfound awareness that, despite all we've achieved, we can no longer rely on government or institutions to make the world an equal or better place for us. We have to rely on ourselves. So get going. Flip through, pick your issues—the ones that really hit home and matter to you—and start reshaping the future, for yourself, your mother, your daughters, and their daughters.

As you browse through this book, remember you don't have to do it *all*. Happily, there are 93 million women over the age of eighteen in America—and in total we make up 52 percent of our country's population. With numbers like these, and with *each* of us just doing one or two of these five-minute, "simple things," we possess the strength and power to create wide-scale solutions that will make the world a better place for all women in the nineties. And beyond.

WHERE WOMEN
ARE RIGHT NOW

· · · · ·

Family Leave and
Child Care
• • • • •

Compare . . .

"European Community nations have agreed to guarantee women 14 weeks' maternity leave at wages at least equal to the sick pay offered in their countries. . . . The accord, to take effect Jan. 1, 1993, will mainly benefit women in Britain, Ireland and Portugal. The other nine member nations already guarantee at least 14 weeks' pregnancy leave at wages higher than sick pay, some at full pay."—*The New York Times*, November 1991

"In Sweden either parent is eligible to take a one-year *paid* leave after the birth or adoption of a baby. In France paid leave is [14 weeks] and mothers (or fathers) employed by large firms are also guaranteed *two years* of unpaid leave."—*New Woman*, February 1992

. . . and Contrast

"George Bush, who campaigned on a profamily platform, vetoed one of the few pieces of profamily legislation to pass both houses of Congress, last year's Family and Medical Leave Act. The act, minimal by other countries' standards, would have guaranteed twelve weeks of unpaid family-related leave a year, with health insurance and job security, to workers in firms with more than fifty employees. (Bush is expected to veto the bill again if it passes this year.)"—*Vogue*, September 1991

"Bush Refuses to Aid Families: Homey Rhetoric Conceals Callous, Indifferent Policy: . . . As for Barbara, well: We like you,

2

Barbara! But you're sleeping with the enemy."—Ellen Goodman, syndicated columnist, *The Boston Globe*, February 1992

And Yet

"According to a study conducted by economics professors at Cornell University and the University of Connecticut, the costs of allowing such leaves for most workers is less than letting them quit and hiring permanent replacements."—*Fortune*, May 1991

Sexual Harassment
•••••

The Good

"One happy side effect [after the Senate's hearings of Anita Hill during the Judge Clarence Thomas confirmation was] the Senate's sudden decision that they should live with the civil rights laws of the land. . . . The senators voted to allow their very own employees to sue them for things like, uh, sexual harassment."—Ellen Goodman, syndicated columnist, *The Boston Globe,* November 1991

The bad . . .

"If women [who say they were harassed] are composed, people say that what they are claiming must not have happened. If they are emotional, they say, 'You can't believe her; she's a hysterical woman.' And even though Anita Hill was composed, they said she was hysterical."—*U.S. News & World Report,* end of year issue, December 1991/January 1992

. . . and the Ugly

"As resentment toward women's growing presence in the workplace mounted in the course of the '80s, so did the many measures of hostility to women in the workplace. Charges of sexual harassment filed at the EEOC nearly doubled in the decade. Yet the EEOC's public affairs office saw, heard and reported no evil. In the late '80s, the agency even advised inquiring journalists that sexual harassment charges were on the wane. . . . By 1987 . . . the EEOC district offices and state equal employment agencies were closing 40% to 80% of their cases without proper, or any, investigation."—*The Wall Street Journal*, October 1991

The Disturbing

"The Bush administration . . . opposed the [recent bill which passed, allowing students who are sexually harassed to win money damages from schools that receive federal funds], warning that providing for money damages could expose schools to 'potentially massive financial liability.' "—*The Washington Post*, February 1992

What Does Anita Think?

"[Our] sense of powerlessness is particularly troubling when one observes the research that says individuals with graduate education experience more harassment than do persons with less than a high school diploma. The message: when you try to obtain power through education, the beast harassment responds by striking more often and more vehemently."—Anita Hill, *Ms.*, January/February 1992

Every Woman's Right To Choose

• • • • •

Going . . .

". . . the only doctor [left] in South Dakota who performs abortions works in a cinderblock office with bullet-proof windows and burglar alarms . . . for 11 years he has had to walk through pickets to enter his office."—*The New York Times*, March 1992

Going . . .

Abortions are already so hard to come by some women are resorting to illegal abortions—and dying. "Rosie Jimenez, a 27-year-old single mother on a college scholarship, had six months to go before completing her teaching credentials when she discovered she was pregnant. She had to cross the border to Mexico to find abortion services she could afford. The cheap, illegal abortion killed her."—Susan Faludi, *Backlash*, 1991

. . . Gone?

If the Supreme Court overturns Roe *v.* Wade: "Congress is unlikely to pass a national abortion law . . . because its political fallout is dicey. Members will lavish oratory in favor of or against the Supreme Court's overruling, but ultimately conclude that abortion rights should be left in the hands of the individual states."—*Insight*, February 1992

Who *Can't* We Count On to Protect Our Right to Choose?

" '[Dan] Quayle thinks he can finesse the abortion issue and "railroad the platform through," ' [one] senator said. 'You avoid [a fight] by having so much control over the platform committee that you have a hearing, and let them have their say, and say, "Thank you, ladies," and write what you want.' "—*The Washington Post*, March 1992, in an article on getting an anti-choice platform pushed through at the Republican Convention

During a recent anti-choice rally in Washington, DC, "President Bush encouraged the anti-abortion crowd with a quick pep talk, broadcast over loudspeakers via telephone hookup from the White House to the Mall."—*The Washington Post*, January 1992

Women's Health
● ● ● ● ●

The Problem . . .

"Women constitute 52% of the population and account for about 70% of all [patients], yet they represent only a small fraction of the *decision-making* groups in medical education, training, practice and policy. Even now in the early 1990s, only 5% of all . . . full professors in medical faculty are women, and only 2% of all medical school deans are women."—*Journal of the American Medical Women's Association*, November/December 1990

An Unhealthy Gap

". . . an information gap . . . may be endangering millions of American women. A number of treatments now recommended for men and women—from cholesterol-lowering drugs and diets to AIDS therapies and antidepressants—have been studied almost exclusively in men. Little hard evidence exists about their efficacy or safety for women."—*Time*, special issue, Fall 1990

What We Need Now . . .

Research on women's health issues is badly needed on: "substance abuse during pregnancy; eating disorders [such as] bulimia and anorexia . . . tobacco use . . . the prevention and treatment of osteoporosis [and] on the impact of new reproductive technology. . . . Reproductive health issues, particularly as they affect women, have been neglected greatly."—*Journal of the American Medical Women's Association*, May/June 1991.

Why Things Change So Slowly . . .

"Women of both [political] parties guided the measure [to get mammograms covered by insurance] through their own committees, but one key subcommittee remained an all-male bastion. A female lobbyist who regularly worked that panel volunteered to ask a friendly congressman to introduce the mammogram language. 'I can't do that,' he protested. 'I did the last women's thing, the guys will think I'm soft on women.'"—Cokie Roberts, *The Washington Post*, February 1992

Violence Against Women
• • • • •

The Way It Is . . .

"1991: *The New York Times* publishes a disparaging article on the life of a woman who says she was raped by William Kennedy Smith. 'She had a little wild streak,' reads one anonymous quote."—*Glamour*, March 1992

"The honeymoon period [a group of fraternity brothers from Syracuse told a reporter] is the first few weeks of the school year, when freshmen girls arrive on campus. They are so naive, especially the ones from small towns. . . . And the upperclassmen are there waiting for them. They know how to manipulate the girls . . . what moves to make. . . ."—*Glamour*, September 1990

With Injustice for All . . .

In April 1991, five sons of prominent families in Tampa, Florida, were implicated in the rape of a 22-year-old girl. In March 1992, one of the men was brought to trial for rape but acquitted even after a friend testified they had dosed the woman's beer with LSD, slipped her four hits of acid on a cracker without her knowledge (at which point she seemed to be unconscious), and some of them had engaged in sexual acts with her. The young female victim testified she passed out and upon awakening, "I felt so dirty. They were all laughing at me. They said, 'You were having a good time last night—you enjoyed it.' " *The boy testifying, on the other hand, said his* "fun" *was marred only when a nightstand belonging to his parents was broken.* "That's what I was worried about," *he said.—Los Angeles Times*, March 1992

July 1991: "Three St. John's University, Long Island, students were acquitted of charges of sodomy and rape, in spite of testimony against them by fellow lacrosse team members. The jurors complained that the plaintiff cried on the stand and was unsure how much she drank."—*New Directions for Women*, September/October 1991

Is There Any End in Sight?

September 1991: "The Judicial Conference of the United States [opposed] legislation that would create a civil-rights remedy for victims of sex assaults. The bill, called the Violence Against Women Act, declares that rape is a bias or hate crime and allows victims to recover compensatory and punitive damages in federal court. [But] the Judicial Conference . . . voted unanimously . . . to oppose the act because it would add too many cases to the federal courts."—*American Bar Association Journal*, December 1991

Sexism in the Media
• • • • •

Sexy or Sexist?

In the Print Media:

   —*In June 1990*, Esquire *runs a cover story entitled "Your Wife: An Owner's Manual." Their pictorial shows a "wife" divided down the middle, one side of her lower half aproned and captioned by: "Her apron strings: Do they tie her down?" The other side shows a sketch of a sink's plumbing drawn over her uterus, captioned with: "Her plumbing: How much should you know?"*

In Television Advertising:

   —*In 1991, Stroh Brewery advertises its Old Milwaukee beer by having a scantily clad, buxom "Swedish Bikini Team" drop half-naked from the sky, over a group of men who are fishing, to attest that: "It doesn't get any better than this."*

   —*In a recent Coors Light beer commercial, meant to encourage women to buy light beer, a woman in a scant bikini walks seductively across the beach as the announcer says: "Coors Light. Because if you don't watch your figure, who will?"*

   —*A 1991 campaign for Bud Dry beer includes a commercial in which the announcer asks: "Why do gentlemen prefer blondes?" As the camera pans up and down the body of a long-legged, curvaceous blonde in a short, skin-tight skirt, the answer flashes on the screen: "Dumb question."*

Sexism or Sadism?

Fashion ads during the 1980s showed: "a woman lying on an ironing board while a man applied an iron to her crotch (Esprit); a woman in a straitjacket (Seruchi); a woman dangling by her legs, chicken-style, from a man's fist ('Cotlers—For the Right Stance,' the ad read), and a woman knocked to the floor, her shirt ripped open (Foxy Lady)."—Susan Faludi, *Backlash*, 1991

How You Can Make a Difference
·····

1.

Stick a "This Insults Women" Sticker on Sexist Posters and Ads

• • • • •

Ever pass by a blatantly sexist poster or ad displayed on a bus shelter or in a train station and think, "That's so sexist—but what can *I* do about it?" Ask no more. Next time you see a sexist ad (like the one for KIKIT clothing, in which a man drags a woman to him by pulling a fistful of her hair), a poster advertising a new film in which women are slashed, hacked, or raped for viewer's titillation, or a "girlie poster" (like the popular one with "U.S.D.A. Choice" stamped over a girl's naked torso), slap a "This Insults Women" sticker on it, and walk on by. Your message remains behind as an eye-opener for the next passerby. Who might just be male.

Did You Know?

● A recent study shows that in 97% of print ads, a woman is either portrayed in an image that puts her down—for example, as a "dumb blonde," a sex object, or a whimpering victim (73%)—or in a narrow, stereotypical female role such as wife, mother, or secretary (24%).
● Sexist ads which appear on bus sides, bus shelters, and subway walls appear on property that *your* tax dollars help pay to maintain.
● 1 out of 15 Hollywood films has a rape scene.
● Exposure to films showing sexual violence toward women—not just porn films, but widely released, popular R movies—increases men's sexually aggressive behavior toward women on dates, men's acceptance that violence toward women is okay, and their belief in rape myths ("she really likes it").

Five-Minute Solutions:

- Get a set of "This Insults Women" stickers (20 stickers cost only $1.50; see Resources) and carry a few in your wallet so you'll have one ready the next time you're strolling along and suddenly notice a demeaning advertisement, poster, or movie ad. The handy thing about these stickers is that they're no bigger than the palm of your hand, and because it takes only seconds to put one on a poster or ad, you don't have to be concerned about being challenged by a passer-by. So, take a few seconds next time you see a sexist image and "stick it to it." (A second sticker is also available which says, "This Promotes Women Hating.")
- Write to the Trader's Truck Accessories, 2652 Pacific Park Drive, Whittier, CA 90601, and ask them to stop distributing their naked lady mud-flap decals, which truckers affix to their rear-wheel mud flaps so that all of us driving behind them get to gaze at crude profiles of nude, reclining females.

Resources:

Order your "This Insults Women" stickers through: Donnelly/Colt, Box 188, Hampton, CT 06247. Or call: (203) 455-9621. 20 stickers cost $1.50, and 1000 stickers cost $32. Send a check with your order. Sorry, no credit cards.

Warning: The Media May Be Hazardous to Your Health is a wonderful video which illustrates how the media objectifies women in movies and ads. It rents for $40 a week plus $5 shipping from Media Watch, P.O. Box 618, Santa Cruz, CA 95061-0618; (408) 423-6355.

2.
Stop Tobacco Companies from Targeting Women
• • • • •

As tobacco companies lose revenues because so many smokers are kicking the habit, they're increasingly targeting young *women*, who they see as the most promising new market to replace traditionally older, male smokers. Meanwhile, although new cases of lung cancer among men have leveled off in recent years, the number of cases in women since 1980 has more than doubled. It seems the only equality that smoking has given women is that we are now getting lung cancer at a higher rate than men.

Did You Know?

- During the last five years, lung cancer has surpassed breast cancer as the number-one cancer killer of women.
- At the current rate, tobacco-related deaths among women worldwide will more than double by the year 2020—and well over a million adult women will die each year from tobacco-related illnesses.
- 20% of young women now graduating from high school smoke, versus 10% of young men.
- According to a new study, the more money a magazine makes off cigarette advertising, the less likely it is to report on the dangers of smoking.
- Proportionately more cigarette ads are placed in women's magazines than in other publications.

Five-Minute Solutions:

- Encourage magazines that either don't carry cigarette ads or that take tough stands on smoking by subscribing and/or writing to the editor and telling her or him you appreciate being given the honest scoop. (You can find the editor's name and the address on the masthead or contents page.) Editors need to be encouraged by readers, because in order to give you the honest scoop, they may be taking the risk of losing big-spending cigarette advertisers (the tobacco industry spends $3 billion a year on advertising—the equivalent of $100 a second). (By the way, never jot a note on a subscription card; while that may seem like a quick way to share your thoughts with editors, it's useless; subscription cards usually go to an entirely different town and state, and no one in editorial ever sees them.)
- Cancel (or don't renew) your subscriptions to magazines which carry ads (or especially editorials) promoting smoking for women. When you stop subscribing, write a postcard to the editor, telling her or him why you felt you had to cancel. Lack of subscribers means lack of revenue—and revenues affect the bottom line.

Resources:

For more information, contact The Smoking Control Advocacy Resource Center, Advocacy Institute; (202) 659-8475; 1730 Rhode Island Ave., NW, #600, Washington, DC 20036-3118.

You can also get the facts (including the Surgeon General's Report) from the Office of Smoking and Health, Centers for Disease Control, 1600 Clifton Rd. NE, Mail Stop K50, Atlanta, GA 30333; (404) 488-5705.

If you're currently a smoker, get *Women Smokers Can Quit: A Different Approach,* by Sue F. Delaney, from Women's Healthcare Press ($6.95): (800) 543-3854; 500 Davis St. #700, Evanston, IL 60201. Then take her advice.

3.

Start a Phone Tree—for Family-Friendly Laws

•••••

By now you're probably well aware that among all industrialized nations, America has the worst policies (meaning none) for parents when it comes to family leave and child care. But that can change: you can have a profound impact on family leave and child care laws *right before* they come up for vote by spending just five minutes on the phone with a few friends—and Capitol Hill. The secret: a free, valuable resource, coupled with the "phone tree" approach.

Did You Know?

- Two thirds of mothers with young children are in the workforce.
- 51% of moms with newborns return to work before their baby's first birthday.
- 87% of our nation's 50 million working women are likely to become pregnant at some point in their careers.
- 127 countries, including Japan and all European nations, require maternal or parental leave for employees. Who doesn't? America and South Africa.
- As of this writing, George Bush has threatened to veto for a *second* time the Family and Medical Leave Act—which would guarantee 12 weeks of unpaid family-related leave a year to workers in firms with over 50 employees.
- It will take two thirds of our representatives in Congress to stand behind this bill to override a presidential veto—so we must continue to show Congress our unbridled support for this legislation.

Five-Minute Solutions:

● Find out where family leave and child care laws stand right now:
1. Call the Children's Defense Fund (CDF) legislative hotline at (202) 662-3678 for their one-minute update on where Family Leave and other child care legislation stands this week in Congress.
2. For the latest information on the Family and Medical Leave Act (FMLA), call the Work and Family Department at the Women's Legal Defense Fund (they've led much of the lobbying effort for Family Leave) at (202) 986-2600. (If you want to receive regular, free updates on the bill by mail, ask to be put on their "FMLA Activists List.")

● Now, to make a real impact, join in with a few friends to form a "phone tree." As you keep track of where the Family Leave bill (Senate bill S.5, House bill H.R. 2) and other important family-friendly and child care bills stand, spread the word so other women *also* know when to pick up the phone and tell legislators how they feel. Here's how the phone tree works: if you and just four friends each phone five friends, and they each phone five friends, together you could reach 155 people in 10 minutes. With a second round of calls, you could reach 155 legislators' offices in 10 more minutes. To reach the offices of the House of Representatives, call: (202) 225-3121; the Senate: (202) 224-3121 (before calling, see our "Phone for Action" guidelines in Section 20: Tell One Congressperson How Violence Against Women Has Harmed You, p. 56).

● See the postcard at the end of this book and "Let the President Know."

Resources:

Children's Defense Fund, 25 E Street NW, Washington, DC 20001. Information hotline: (202) 662-3678. Office number: (202) 628-8787.

Women's Legal Defense Fund, 1875 Connecticut Ave, NW, Suite 710, Washington, DC 20009; (202) 986-2600.

4.

Get a Performance Review Before Saying, "I'm Pregnant"

• • • • •

Every year tens of thousands of women who take time off for maternity leave find themselves replaced. Even though pregnancy discrimination is illegal, some employers get away with it—often by saying they've found "better" workers. Vague tactics like these, coupled with a lack of sufficient federal legislation, allow companies to subtly bar women of childbearing years from the best jobs. How do you make sure pregnancy discrimination doesn't happen to you? Before telling your employer you're pregnant, ask for a performance review. If it's a matter of *record* that you're doing a good job, the company will be much less likely to let you go, for fear of legal reprisals.

Did You Know?

- According to 9to5, National Association of Working Women, pregnancy discrimination is the *number-one* complaint on their toll-free Job Problem hotline.
- 70% to 80% of adult, pregnant women work full time.
- Four out of five of these women work into their third trimester.
- 53% of working women do *not* receive any maternity leave benefits from their company.
- Flimsy federal laws require only that pregnant women who need time off from work must be treated the same as employees who take time off because of other medical conditions. So, if a company's medical disability policy is to allow only one week's paid disability leave, then a pregnant woman has *one week* to deliver her baby and get back on the job or be let go.

Five-Minute Solutions:

- If every pregnant woman in America got a performance review before saying, "I'm pregnant," as many as a quarter of a million women might avoid pregnancy discrimination and the loss of their jobs at the very time when they're most vulnerable. (Census Bureau statistics indicate that more than 250,000 women a year are involuntarily let go from their jobs while pregnant.)

- How do you ask for a review out of the blue? Let your boss know you'd like to be sure you're meeting his or her expectations as well as the goals of the corporation—and for that reason, you'd like to get a review of your recent work performance. Many companies have standard procedures for reviews, but if your company doesn't, simply write a memo saying you'd like to check on how you're doing. Outline where *you* feel you stand on various projects, what you feel you've accomplished, and ask your boss to sign off on this memo. Once it's signed, keep it in a file at home, along with previous performance reviews.

- If you're worried about how your company will react when you say, "I'm pregnant," or if you feel you've already been the victim of pregnancy discrimination, call the 9to5 Job Problem Hotline at (800) 522-0925. (You may get a busy signal several times, but be persistent.)

- If you're job hunting and planning on a pregnancy down the line, discreetly inquire about the benefits offered at the company where you're interviewing. Ask about disability leave (many pregnancy leaves last no longer than disability leave, and by law don't have to) as well as family leave policies.

Resources:

Job Survival Hotline, 9to5, National Association of Working Women, 614 Superior Ave., NW, Cleveland, OH 44113. Hotline: (800) 522-0925. Office: (216) 566-9308.

5.

Feel More Secure About Who's Minding Your Kids

• • • • •

Since we live in a country which lacks any kind of across-the-board federal guidelines for child care standards, it can be difficult to feel completely secure after you leave your kids with an in-home sitter, at family day care, or at a day care center. As you drive away waving goodbye in the mornings, you might sometimes wonder, Is my child in the best of hands? (Especially with recent films like *The Hand That Rocks the Cradle* playing into women's fears.) If you worry now and then about who's minding the kids, know this: there *are* systems in place to help you regain your maternal peace of mind.

Did You Know?

- Nearly 5 million children in America under the age of five are entrusted to some type of day care (day care centers, family day care, or in-home sitters).
- Child care workers' wages have declined by 25% since the mid-1970s.
- The average day care worker makes $10,000 a year—a salary beneath the federal poverty line. By comparison, the average beginning salary of an animal keeper at the San Francisco Zoo is $30,000 a year.
- The annual staff turnover rate is 39% among for-profit day care centers.
- Day care studies find: the lower the wages, the higher the turnover, and the higher the turnover, the lower the quality of care for your child.

Five-Minute Solutions:

● Once you use the suggestions and resources below to make sure your child is getting quality care, you'll feel more secure about who's minding your kids—which means you'll spend *less* time and energy worrying about them and have *more* quality, worry-free hours, whether you're with your child or at your desk. And that's critical: excess worry causes burnout, and burnout keeps us from rising to our potential both as good moms at home and as creative women in the workplace. Here's where to turn for the information you need:

1. If your child is being cared for in a family day care home (in another person's house, by a nonrelative), take two minutes and ask your provider whether she or he is registered or licensed. (If so, they'll be able to show you their state registration card.) Although state laws differ, registration and licensing usually means the person watching your child is insured for injury to children and has passed state police and FBI criminal background checks. In some states, unregistered providers are subject to fines of up to $1000.

2. If your child is in a group day care center, find out whether or not that center is licensed. Call the National Association of Child Care Resource and Referral Agency (NACCRRA) (see Resources). They'll give you the phone number for the best *local* Child Care Resource and Referral Agency in your area. That agency will tell you how good the licensing laws in your area are, what requirements day care centers in your state must meet in order to become licensed, as well as whether or not your day care center *is* licensed.

Resources:

National Association of Child Care Resource and Referral Agencies, 2116 Campus Drive SE, Rochester, MN 55904; (507) 287-2220. Get their excellent *Complete Guide to Choosing Child Care* ($12.95), by calling (800) 733-3000. Ask for book # 679-73100-8.

Child Care Action Campaign, 330 Seventh Avenue, 17th Floor, New York, NY 10001; (212) 239-0138; sends members 28 valuable *Information Guides* (including helpful tips on choosing all types of child care, *and* how to use the Federal Child Care Tax Credit). Members (cost: $25) are also kept abreast of pending child care legislation in a bi-monthly newsletter, *Child Care ActioNews*.

6.

Shop for a Better World for Working Moms (and Dads)

• • • • •

A few farsighted corporations are waking up to the needs of American families and offering more family-friendly options like parental leave and help with child care. But most American corporations lag light-years behind the needs of today's working parents. How can you send a strong message—one which will be *heard* by big corporations—so they'll start family-friendly programs? The more we shop for brand-name items made by companies who give working moms a fair shake, the more we affect the bottom-line profits of corporate America, and the faster change happens.

Did You Know?

- Only 11% of American corporations with 10 or more employees offer employer-sponsored child day care or financial assistance toward child care.
- 60% of corporations with 50 or more employees *do not* offer any flexible parental leave options.
- A recent study done by the U.S. Small Business Administration found: "the net cost to employers of placing workers on leave is always substantially smaller than the cost of terminating an employee."
- In four states where family/medical leave is being implemented, an overwhelming 91% of employers reported that they had no problems or significant increase in costs after implementing new leave policies.

Five-Minute Solutions:

- Buy brand-name products made by companies that *have* family-friendly policies (and avoid products made by companies that *don't*). Call or send for the guide *Shopping for a Better World* (800-729-4CEP). This handbook rates 166 companies on 10 key issues—including each company's family-friendly policies and day care benefits. Some big winners? Kodak; Johnson & Johnson (Tylenol, Band-Aid); Procter & Gamble (Crest, Duncan Hines); and Hershey (Kit-Kat, Cadbury). When you order the guide, also request their free list showing which companies make exactly which brand-name products. So, next time you need disposable diapers, buy family-friendly Procter & Gamble's Pampers (not Kimberly-Clark's Huggies). Need peanut butter? Buy Procter & Gamble's Jif (skip Con-Agra's Peter Pan).

- Get *Working Mother* magazine's annual survey of *The Best Companies for Working Mothers,* published every October (Special Projects Dept., 230 Park Avenue, New York, NY 10169; (212) 551-9385. Cost per reprint: $1.25). This handy guide names 85 major corporations, explains what products they manufacture or produce, and tells why they're good companies for working moms.

Resources:

The Council on Economic Priorities (CEP), 30 Irving Place, New York, NY 10003-9990; (800) 729-4CEP; puts out *Shopping for a Better World* ($7.49). Inquire about their Spring 1993 guide to help students shop for a better world which will cover brand-name clothes, tapes, CDs, etc.

"Managing Smart," a free brochure put out by The Families and Work Institute (FWI), 330 Seventh Avenue, New York, NY 10001, (212) 465-2044 or (212) 465-8637, details their management training program which has helped companies like Johnson & Johnson rise to the A-list of family-friendly corporations. Drop it in the suggestion box at *your* workplace.

The *DCAP Handbook: A How-to Manual for Employers and Employees on the Dependent Care Assistance Program* lays out everything your company needs to know to help them set aside *pre-tax* dollars (up to $5000 a year) to help *you* pay for child care. Drop the free brochure on their handbook into the office suggestion box, too (handbook: $35 plus $3 shipping), MASSPIRG Education Fund, 29 Temple Place, Boston, MA 02111, (617) 292-4800.

III. Sexual Harassment and Sexist Comments

7.

Post a Poster on Harassment
• • • • •

Ever since Justice Clarence Thomas was accused of sexual harassment—yet the Senate confirmed him for the Supreme Court anyway—many women have felt they'd better just keep quiet about being harassed because no one will believe them. *Forbes* magazine even recently called sexual harassment an overblown, "phony" issue. But if you've ever been harassed, you know that it remains a common, serious problem. To help make everyone clear about exactly what sexual harassment is and what can be done about it, get the poster mentioned below and post it at your office.

Did You Know?

- 22,619,200 to 49,762,240 women in this country have been sexually harassed.
- In 95% of cases, the woman didn't even tell a co-worker, let alone file a formal complaint.
- Sexual harassment costs the average Fortune 500 company $6.7 million a year in absenteeism, low productivity, and employee turnover.
- If every woman in the U.S. who has ever been harassed sent an anonymous one-page account of her story to the EEOC, the EEOC would receive approximately 500 tons of mail. Laid end to end, the letters would stretch from New York to Hong Kong.

How to Make a Difference:

- Obtain the poster "Sexual Harassment in Our Workplace: Your Legal Rights" ($2.50, address below) and post it near your desk at work.
- Given a choice between two equally good job offers, go with the company that employs the most women. Why? Harassment rates at companies where women make up less than 25% of the workforce are twice as high as they are in companies that are over 50% female.
- If you have more time and a personal story to tell, send that letter. The address: EEOC, 1801 L Street NW, Washington, DC 20507.
- Encourage your company to set up a harassment grievance procedure if it doesn't yet have one. Write for *The 9to5 Guide to Combatting Sexual Harassment,* available for $9.95 from: 9to5, National Association of Working Women, 614 Superior Ave. NW, Cleveland, OH 44113; (216) 566-9308. If you prefer not to approach your company directly, you can simply drop this guide in the office suggestion box.

Resources:

The Women's Legal Defense Fund, 1875 Connecticut Ave. NW, Suite 710, Washington, DC 20009, (202) 986-2600, has the poster mentioned above, and the helpful guide *Sexual Discrimination in the Workplace: Your Legal Rights ($7.95).*

8.

React Fast If
You're Harassed
• • • • •

Even after all the attention about harassment in recent headlines, many men continue to see harassment as harmless. Their attitude often seems to be that women are "making too much of a little office bantering." But, as women know, sexual harassment, which is really about power, can intimidate a woman, keep her from doing her best work, and, in some cases, make her feel so threatened she quits. If you're harassed, don't wait for it to happen again or get worse before you try to put a stop to it. Use the guidelines below (the ones that fit your situation)—and make it clear from the start that sexual innuendoes and approaches are unacceptable.

Did You Know?

- Men and women have different reactions to sexual advances in the office. In one study, 67% of men—but only 17% of women—said they'd be flattered by a sexual proposition from a co-worker.
- By comparison, only 15% of men—but 63% of women—said they'd be insulted by a sexual proposition from a co-worker.
- Women aren't crying wolf; 64% of human-resources executives in Fortune 500 firms say most complaints of sexual harassment are valid.

How to Make a Difference:

A strategy that works to solve the problem on one job could get you fired from another. So use the tips below (suggested by sexual harassment attorneys and women's groups) coupled with your best judgment.

- If you're unclear about whether or not what was said or done was sexual harassment, ask yourself, "Was this an unwelcome sexual remark this same man would have made to a woman who was his superior? Or to his mother, daughter, aunt, wife, or grandmother . . ." (you get the picture).
- The minute a man acts offensively, speak up (if possible, where others can hear). What should you say? Try deflecting obscene sexual remarks with one of these three questions in a voice that makes it painfully obvious you are not encouraging his behavior: (1) Why do you ask? (2) What makes you say that? or (3) Would you repeat that? Example: When a man says, "I know you've thought about sleeping with me," you might looked stunned and reply, "Would you repeat that?"
- Also pay attention to your body language whenever you speak to this man (say he asks you out for a drink, and you respond, "I'm comfortable with our relationship the way it is and wouldn't feel comfortable taking it further, even for drinks"). Look directly at him in a confident manner (don't hunch your shoulders or look away or wring your hands), and stand at a distance that is neither so close as to be intimate nor so far away as to give the impression that you're intimidated.
- If the problem persists, photocopy records of your work performance (in case you should need them in the future, for another job interview).
- Buy a small notebook and keep a written record of all harassing behavior. Jot down what happened, how you responded, if you had witnesses, who you told. Keep the notebook at home, not at work.
- Tell friends and co-workers. If other women are being harassed, too, join forces. There is power in numbers.
- Write the harasser a memo or letter saying: "Dear Joe: This is what you did and why it bothers me. Please don't do it anymore." Keep a copy in your home files.
- If the problem continues and your company or union has a grievance procedure, use it. Document every step by writing memos and making notes, describing precisely what happened, with dates and times.
- As a last resort, file a complaint with your state equal employment opportunity or human rights commission or the federal EEOC.

Resources:

Call 9to5, National Association of Working Women; they have a sexual harassment hotline: 1-800-522-0925 (Mon.–Fri., 10:00 A.M. to 4:00 P.M. ET).

In Case of Sexual Harassment . . . A Guide for Women Students, $4 from: Center for Women Policy Studies, 2000 P Street NW, Suite 508, Washington, DC 20036; (202) 872-1770.

9.

Don't Ignore Sexist Slurs Spoken by the Men You Know
• • • • •

Now and then most of us encounter a wayward sexist comment from a man we care about. A father, lover, brother, co-worker, or son. We hear a spouse mutter, "Women can't drive," or a male co-worker say, "Women like my boss must not be getting enough sex." But because we are fond of him (and don't want to offend, start an argument, or make him think we're a boot-stomping man-hater), we often let such comments slide by. Unfortunately, whether these comments come out in the form of lighthearted jokes, slurs, innuendoes, or putdowns of women in general, not responding to them can make men think we find them acceptable—which only perpetuates them.

Did You Know?

- A recent survey found that men admit to making secret, sexist assumptions once every two and a half days. (And that's only what they *admit* to!)
- If all the adult men in America had to pay $1 for every sexist thought they admit to having, at the end of one year their collective tab would total $11 billion.
- Over half of working women say they've suffered unpleasant incidents at work due to off-color sexual jokes and demeaning comments about women.
- 84% of women say they find men's sexual jokes in the workplace unacceptable.

Five-Minute Solutions:

- When a man you care for makes a sexist comment ("I guess if today's meeting doesn't go her way, she'll cry," or "I bet that's a woman driving," or "Sexual harassment shouldn't be outlawed, it should just be graded from excellent to poor,") and expects you not to mind, tell him (in a nonblaming way) that you do. You might say something like: "I know you don't mean any harm by it. And I know we all harbor some sexist thoughts since we were raised in a sexist society. But I feel uncomfortable when you make sexist remarks." If you're in a relationship with this man, you might also add, "One of the things I value about our relationship is that we're very loving toward one another. But I feel less loving toward you when you make disparaging remarks about women." Unless we constantly enlighten men—even if only with small reminders like these—this sort of sexist commentary will never go away and things will never change.

- If you're in a group or with a man who makes a sexist joke, don't join in the laughter. Anyone who has seen clips of women in audiences watching Andrew Dice Clay when he did his woman-hating schtick knows that women often go along with group laughter at sexist humor, especially when the man they're with is enjoying himself. But letting a man think you find putdowns of women acceptable (even if they're disguised in humor) only sends the message that it's okay in *your* mind. Next time you hear a sexist joke, tell the man (or woman) who told it you are not amused, and why.

- If a stranger makes a sexist remark as you're walking down the street (say a guy yells out, "This girl's got legs!" or "Oh come on, give us a smile," or worse, "Nice tomatoes!"), don't smile to placate him. If you do, it may give the false impression that you find this kind of uninvited attention flattering. It is *not* flattery (street harassers are generally not very finicky) and catcalling is about exerting power, not giving compliments. (We all know what it's like to grow afraid as we approach a group of guys hanging out on a street corner, ogling us as we get closer . . . in such a moment, they have the power, not us.) Moreover, when you think about it, it's not a very long stretch of the hand from this kind of unwanted verbal harassment on the street to an unwanted sexual assault in a dark doorway.

10.
Let Your Fingers Do the Walking
● ● ● ● ●

I t's no secret that despite all the progress we've made, full-time working women still make less than three quarters for every $1 men earn, and female college graduates still make less than men with only a high school diploma. A growing number of women feel we can best correct this inequity by going into business for ourselves. Every time you patronize a woman-owned business, you're giving women more economic power. How to find them? The next time you need your carpets cleaned, a business card printed, or a clogged sink repaired, check the new Women's Yellow Pages. Then do business with a female entrepreneur.

Did You Know?

- Between 1982 and 1987, the number of women-owned businesses rose from 2,612,621 to 4,112,787—an increase of about 58%.
- Women are creating new businesses at twice the rate of men. In the past 15 years alone, more than 7 million women have launched new businesses which contribute more than $278 billion to the nation's economy.
- Yet to succeed long term, a female entrepreneur needs all the support she can get: 65% of all new businesses fail within five years.

Five-Minute Solutions:

- Twenty-one cities and regions around the country now have companies that publish Women's Yellow Pages—just like phone directo-

31

ries, except women own 99% of the businesses listed. So, the next time you need a podiatrist, plumber, judo teacher, or house painter, let your fingers do the walking—to a woman-owned business.

● Below we've listed the Women's Yellow Pages available when we went to press. But more are being published all the time (unfortunately, some also go out of business). So, if your town isn't listed or if you have any trouble reaching one of the numbers below, find out if this service is available in your area by contacting the National Association of Women's Yellow Pages, 7358 N. Lincoln Ave., Suite 150, Chicago, IL 60646; 708-679-7800

ALABAMA (Mobile): 205-473-5320; ARIZONA (Phoenix): 602-945-5000; CALIFORNIA (Monterey, Santa Cruz, and San Benito counties): 408-455-0564, (Los Angeles and Orange counties): 310-398-5761; (San Diego): 619-294-9918; GEORGIA (Greater Atlanta): 404-772-0050; ILLINOIS (Chicago): 708-679-7800; INDIANA (Northwestern Indiana): 219-736-8913; KANSAS/MISSOURI (Greater Kansas City): 913-341-4940; LOUISIANA (the state): 318-233-5075; MARYLAND (the state): 410-267-0886; MASSACHUSETTS (Boston): 617-545-9141; NEW MEXICO (Albuquerque): 505-821-1393; NEW YORK (Upper New York State): 716-839-0855; OHIO (Cleveland): 216-449-1371; OKLAHOMA (Oklahoma City): 405-524-7020; OREGON (Portland): 503-223-9344; PENNSYLVANIA (Philadelphia): 215-446-4747; VIRGINIA (Richmond): 804-270-4263; WASHINGTON (Puget Sound area): 206-726-9687; WISCONSIN (Milwaukee): 414-789-1346. Cost per book: between $6 and $12.

Resources:

If you're a female entrepreneur trying to sell to other women, get *Marketing to Women* (33 Broad St., Boston, MA 02109-9612; [(617) 723-4337]). Subscribers get their monthly newsletter and their fantastic yearly *Compendium of Trends,* a review of over 300 key topics of concern to women marketers and female consumers. While it's very expensive ($229) and too costly for individuals, it's not too expensive for a company.

11.
Shop from Women Who
Work at Home
• • • • •

In this half-liberated age when women have to work a double day (one at the office, another at home) and child care policies don't begin to meet a working mother's needs, more and more women are seeking an alternative to the rat race: they're starting businesses at home. This way they can earn money and still take care of their child if she or he gets the flu—without having to explain why they took the day off. Make the world better for these women: buy their products and services whenever you can. Once you get into the home business network, who knows? You may even want to try this route yourself.

Did You Know?

- 11.8 million Americans now earn their livings by working full time at home, and another 26.6 million earn some money at home by working part-time.
- Estimates vary, but anywhere from 46% to 70% of home-based businesses in the U.S. are owned by women.
- Over half of families with a home business have children under eighteen.

How to Make a Difference:

- Support entrepreneurial women at home—and help victims of domestic violence, rape, and homelessness at the same time. "The Company of Women" catalogue, 81% of the stock of which is owned by the Rockland Family Shelter for battered women in Rockland,

New York, offers a treasure trove of items perfect for Christmas and birthdays, from notecards benefiting the Global Fund for Women ($10) to a travel mug that says, "Hats Off to the Woman Who Wears Many" ($7.50). All products in the catalogue made by women-owned businesses are marked with a "W." Call 1-800-937-1193 for a free catalogue.

- For women's handcrafted items—from cloth dolls, pottery, and country quilts to homemade jams—shop from: Homeworkers Organized for More Employment (HOME, Inc.), P.O. Box 10, Orland, ME 04472; (207) 469-7961. The dollars you spend here help women who work at home as well as homeless women, men, and children. The catalogue is free.
- To patronize mother-owned businesses throughout the U.S., call Karla Harris (an entrepreneur mother) at 1-800-886-1550 and ask to be put on her mailing list for the *Mothers Resource Guide*. This $3-a-year information-packed circular includes handy lists of publications, toll-free hotlines, and support groups for mothers at home (including business owners). It also has a small but growing Mother-Owned Business Directory, telling you where you can buy items from toys to T-shirts—all of them literally "home" made.

Resources:

If you're considering starting a home business yourself, two helpful newsletters are the *National Home Business Report* (available from: National Home Business Network, P.O. Box 2137, Naperville, IL 60567; [708] 717-0488) and *Homeworking Mothers* (from Mother's Home Business Network, Box 423, East Meadow, NY 11554; [516] 997-7394).

12.

Go with Headhunters Who Help Break the Glass Ceiling

• • • • •

One reason women plateau at lower management levels than men—and hit the "glass ceiling"—is because corporations often don't ask headhunters to include qualified women among their pool of select candidates for top-level jobs. Most headhunters—nearly 78 percent of whom are male—don't push the issue. After all, their job is to please the corporate client, who may not feel "comfortable" casting about outside the old boy network. Yet many *female* headhunters are now searching out and pushing for talented women candidates. These "top gun" women headhunters are helping to alter the mostly male makeup of today's corporate boardrooms. If you're a candidate for upper management positions, let them know.

Did You Know?

- Women comprise nearly half the workforce, yet hold only 3% of top management positions among Fortune 500 corporations.
- The number of women in top executive positions at America's 1000 largest corporations has increased only 4.5% in more than a *decade*.
- A recent study of male and female managers found that women tend to share power and information and try to enhance their employees' sense of self-worth, whereas men tend to use their positions of power to reward or punish employees based on bottom-line performance.
- The same study found that women's "nontraditional" leadership style "can increase an organization's chances of surviving in an uncertain world, since innovative measures are often what are needed to keep a company afloat dining tough economic times."

What You Can Do:

- If you're as qualified for top management positions as your male colleagues are, yet the corporate climate at work is such that women don't seem to get an equal shot at top jobs, take a minute and send your résumé to one or more top female headhunters who, as a group, often make an extra effort to place women in executive spots. This isn't to say that there aren't men out there who do a good job for women, too; it's just that women headhunters often tell corporations the story *behind* a woman's résumé. (For instance: "On her résumé it looks like she wasn't getting promoted for a five-year stretch, but during those years she had triplets and still excelled at a high-pressure management job." Or, "While she didn't make junior vice president as quickly as this male candidate you're also considering did, bear in mind that she was working at a company which had never had a female junior vice president until she achieved that position— so no wonder it took her longer.") In short, women are often better at understanding other women's struggles, and hence they're often better at showing the whole person behind the "paper story" when presenting female candidates to corporate clients.

- Order the superb guide, *Key Women in Executive Search* (Kennedy Publications: 1-800-531-0007; $10), which lists 100 top female headhunters by the following criteria. Almost all either have their own firms or are partners in firms (so they already carry a lot of clout with corporations); most belong to the Association of Executive Search Consultants (membership mandates adhering to a high code of ethics); and all are with *retainer* search firms as opposed to contingency firms. Why is the latter important? Because headhunters with retainer firms are paid by corporations for their overall good judgment and advice (which in this case may include, "Give this *woman* a chance)," whereas headhunters with contingency firms get fees only if they make a placement (so they may be less likely to push for candidates they don't think the company will readily go for).

- Select the headhunters who specialize in your field and target a few of them. Top headhunters suggest sending a short letter which quickly covers: the kind of executive job you're looking for; whether or not you're willing to move; and your salary requirements. Make it clear you're *not* requesting an interview (retainer firms don't work that way—they come to you when they have something you might be right for, so asking for an interview could make you seem naive). Try ending your letter with: "Should you be working on an assignment for which I might be appropriate, please contact me." Attach your résumé. Send an updated letter and résumé off again every six months, since most firms purge their files twice a year.

Resources:

Key Women in Executive Search, Kennedy Publications, Templeton Rd., Fitzwilliam, NH 03447; 1-800-531-0007 (booklet with select names of high achieving women in the executive search field; $10).

DataLine—The Glass Ceiling, a monthly newsletter which addresses why the glass ceiling exists and what you can do to break through it. $40 a year, 848 California Street, San Francisco, CA 94108; (415) 772-8939.

The Association of Executive Search Consultants can tell you if a female headhunter you're curious about is a member: 230 Park Avenue, Suite 1549, New York, NY 10169; (212) 949-9556.

The International Association of Corporate & Professional Recruiters, Inc., has a membership of 250 search firms and 220 recruiters within major corporations: 4000 Woodstone Way, Louisville, KY 40241; (502) 228-4500.

13.

Make Sure You "Prep" for Your Post-Working Years
• • • • •

W hen most of us see an elderly woman, say, ahead of us in line at the grocery store slowly counting out her change or even handing food stamps to the cashier, we like to think her impoverished state could never befall us or any older woman we know and care for. Yet sadly, three out of four of the elderly poor in the U.S. are *women*. Between a Social Security system that penalizes working women who temporarily leave the workforce to take care of children, and women's lower wages throughout their lives, many women find that they retire into unexpected and full-fledged financial hardship. Short of changing the system overnight, what can you do? Utilize the recently established "PREP" programs now in place for women (no matter what your age) to help ensure your post-paycheck years aren't financially ruinous, but enriching.

Did You Know?

- Older women outnumber older men by three to two.
- 50% of women now working do *not* have a pension plan.
- 80% of retired women are not eligible for pension benefits.
- The average income for women over 65 (from all sources, including Social Security) is $7,300.
- 7 in 10 baby-boom women will outlive their husbands and can expect to be widows for at least 15 years.
- Even many women who work full-time throughout their lives will still fall slightly short of the 35 years of paid full-time work needed to qualify for full Social Security benefits upon their retirement—

often because women are the ones who take temporary breaks from the workforce to care for children.

- Retired women receive, on average, only 76 cents from Social Security for every dollar paid to retired male workers.

What You Can Do:

- Find out exactly how much Social Security you'll be entitled to when you retire by calling 1-800-772-1213 and requesting your Earnings and Benefit Estimate Statement forms. When you receive them take a few minutes to fill out these forms and mail them back to Social Security—they'll then tell you the total wages that have been credited to you annually, the number of work credits you've earned to date, your estimated monthly benefits to date, and an estimate of the Social Security benefits you've already paid. Experts recommend doing this every three years, preretirement. It's especially important if you have moved in and out of the workforce (even if only briefly) to check your accounts and be sure the government has credited all your years of work.

- No matter what age you are, you can begin now to protect yourself financially for your retirement years by making use of the resources available through the "Pre-Retirement Education and Planning for Women" (PREP) Project at the National Center for Women and Retirement Research, Long Island University, Southampton, NY 11968, 1-800-426-7386. Started in 1986 through a federal grant, PREP's goal is to provide women with knowledge and skills to help them better plan for financial security in their later years, and thus eliminate the bleak economic conditions many older women face. Ask if there is a PREP seminar coming to your area (the maximum cost of a seminar is about $25), or inquire about their excellent "PREP Talk for Women" handbooks, which cover much of the same material as their seminars do, such as: "Looking Ahead to Your Financial Future," "Employment and Retirement Issues for Women," and "Social and Emotional Issues for Mid-Life Women" ($10.95 each).

- Give the gift of the helpful and informative video *Women and Money—Things Your Mother Never Told You About Finances* ($29.95 plus $4 shipping, available through PREP) to one older woman near and dear to you. It enlightens those of us who aren't as financially literate as we need to be if we're to have a financially secure lifestyle, postretirement, with little-known information on Social Security benefits, pension plans, vesting rights, and details exactly what happens to your IRA money when you retire. (If the woman you're giving this gift to is already somewhat financially savvy, she may want to fast-forward to the discussion on Social Security, as the first part of the video moves slowly through more rudimentary details.)

● If you have more time, sit down and watch this video *yourself*.

Resources:

The Older Women's League, 666 11th Street NW, Suite 700, Washington, DC 20001, (202) 783-6686, is a national organization dedicated to achieving social, political, and economic equity for midlife and older women. They have an extensive list of reports and publications available. Cost of membership (which includes their bi-monthly newsletter, *The OWL Observer*): $15 a year.

Hotflash, a newsletter put out by the National Action Forum for Midlife and Older Women, works to educate and empower women over 40 on social, physical, and self-esteem issues. Cost: $25 a year for members, P.O. Box 816, Stony Brook, NY 11790-0609.

The Women's Initiative Publications List, D12988, American Association of Retired Persons, AARP Fulfillment, 601 E Street NW, Washington, DC 20049, (202) 434-2277, provides vital information packets emphasizing economic issues for older women.

14.

Don't Let Schools Shortchange Girls in Class

• • • • •

Little boys are more likely to misbehave and have learning problems than little girls, which means they sometimes *need* more disciplining and attention from teachers. But unfortunately, after a while, focusing on boys becomes such a well-ingrained habit for teachers that they end up shortchanging girls in school. According to a large body of new research, teachers from preschool through high school give boys more attention and praise. Teachers often aren't aware of their behavior yet need to be: this pattern in which males get more encouragement, coupled with the fact that textbooks and lessons still often omit women from the pages of history, means girls begin to learn one thing above all else: that their "place" is second to males. Make sure that isn't what *your* daughter is learning in school.

Did You Know?

- When boys call out in class—which they do eight times more often than girls do—teachers listen. But when girls call out, they're usually disciplined ("Raise your hand if you want to speak," etc.).
- Bright girls are usually the most ignored because they tend to be quiet, well behaved, and undemanding.
- Even when boys *don't* volunteer, teachers are more likely to call on them.
- In college, even when boys make up just one to two ninths of a seminar, they do one third to one half of the talking.
- Women in co-ed college classrooms are half as likely to be called on as the men.

- The vast majority of authors and role models studied in classes are male.

How to Make a Difference:

- Call the president (or other officer) of your local Parent Teachers Association (PTA) (if you're not a member of the PTA, get the number from the school nearest you) and suggest getting the new film *Shortchanging Girls, Shortchanging America*, which highlights the gender bias that pervades American schools even in the 1990s. Propose the PTA show the film to parents, teachers, the principal, and the school board. (While the overwhelming number of teachers are women, more than 95% of the nation's school superintendents and 72% of principals are male.) If your PTA asks why the urgency, share the facts above, and explain, too, that studies show awareness training can change the behavior of teachers. This, in turn, raises the confidence level and self-esteem of female students—and that enhances girls' *future* success in life.
- Make your daughter, niece, or granddaughter aware of the women in America's history, since she may not be learning about them in school. Next time a grade school–age girl you care for has a birthday, encourage the theme "Celebrate Women's History." The National Women's History Project has a party kit ($24.95) which includes fun color-in placemats featuring women who've helped shape America's history, from Elizabeth Blackwell to Sally Ride; "Write Women Back into History" pencils; party balloons; and more. Or simply get the birthday girl herself the gift of a *Heroes in Our History Coloring Book* ($4.50), which is full of female historical figures.

Resources:

Shortchanging Girls, Shortchanging America. To order this video (cost: $24.95), call 1-800-225-9998 x90 (the phone rings a long time before being answered and you may be put on hold, but bear with it). American Association of University Women, 1111 16th Street NW, Washington, DC 20036-7731.

For a free catalogue of fun, educational gift ideas, contact the National Women's History Project, 7738 Bell Road, Windsor, CA 95492; (707) 838-6000.

15.

Place a Girl in "Operation Smart"
• • • • •

According to the U.S. Department of Education, girls get better grades than boys do up through high school and throughout college. But their academic prowess and abilities *don't* translate into career success: between the ages of twenty-five and thirty-two, except for those women who studied math in college, more women than men go jobless or take lower-paying jobs (and these are women who *haven't* taken time off to have children). Knowing girls do so well academically, we might ask: Why is it that grown women make up two thirds of all poor adults in America? Facts are, proficiency in math is directly related to a girl's future earning capacity: the ten majors that lead to the highest salaries offered to female college graduates are *all* in math, science, and computer fields. To help boost women's earning power later in life, reduce female poverty and low wages, we need to encourage girls to take math, now. Because our schools *aren't* . . .

Did You Know?

- By third grade, only 37% of girls have used a microscope, compared to 51% of boys.
- A study of science classes found that when teachers needed assistance in carrying out a demonstration, 79% of the time boys were selected to help out.
- Even girls with high grades in math and science are *less* encouraged by teachers to pursue advanced courses in those areas than boys are.

- Between 40% and 45% of women entering college report an interest in majoring in science, but only 15% to 18% actually end up doing so.
- The wage gap between women and men disappears for those women in their early thirties who earned eight or more mathematics credits in college.
- President Bush's 1993 budget proposed eliminating funding for the only federal program aimed at promoting education equity for girls.

Five-Minute Solutions:

- Get one young girl to join Girls Inc.'s "Operation Smart," a free program which helps girls build self-confidence, interest and skills in science, math, and technology by giving them practical experience in using power tools, electrical equipment, and computers. They have more than 200 centers in 122 major cities (see below). Making math and science fun for girls can mean that more girls who are drawn to these fields will *stay* with math and science curriculums later—even if they aren't encouraged to during school hours. This program serves girls from all economic and racial backgrounds. Call Girls Inc. to see if there's an "Operation Smart" near you.
- If you have a little girl, be sure *not* to buy Parker Brothers' "Careers for Girls" game, which lists girls' primary career choices as super-mom and schoolteacher. Instructions include: "Tell us the names of your eight children" and "Burn all your chocolate chip cookies." If the Parker Brothers were the Parker Sisters, perhaps they might have included career options like "rocket scientist" or "chemical engineer." . . . Time it takes you not to buy this game: 0 seconds.

Resources:

Girls Inc. (better known as Girls Clubs), a nonprofit organization, 30 East 33rd Street, New York, NY 10016; (212) 689-3700.

The Clare Boothe Luce Scholarships are given to encourage female college and graduate students, and teachers, to enter, study, graduate in, and teach engineering and science. In the four years since its creation, this foundation has already provided $17 million in scholarships and fellowships to women. If you have an interest in engineering or science, or know someone who does, apply today: 111 West 50th Street, New York, NY 10020; (212) 489-7700.

16.
Stop Saying,
"I Don't Know, But . . ."
•••••

All too often when women express our opinions, we qualify ourselves by saying things like "I don't know, but . . ." or "I'm probably wrong about this, but maybe . . ." Sound familiar? Yet men—who haven't been conditioned to "play dumb" or "play down" their intellect in order to gain acceptance from the opposite sex—are rarely heard using self-deprecating phrases or second-guessing themselves. Next time you're expressing your opinion and are tempted to sound as if you only slightly know what you're talking about, *don't* say, "I don't know."

Did You Know?

- Recent research shows that while eight-, nine-, and ten-year-old girls speak out with frankness and self-assurance, by age twelve or thirteen they begin to pepper their language with self-effacing phrases like "I don't know" or "This is dumb, but . . ."
- Why? Researchers conclude that by age twelve most girls find they have to "cover up" their true opinions, keep quiet, and be nice if they're to preserve the peace in their relationships, fit in, and be liked.
- During these same years, from eight to thirteen, girls' self-esteem plummets.
- In one study, adult men consistently liked and trusted women who spoke self-effacingly more than women who spoke with self-assurance.
- Women, however, *didn't* like other women who used tentative language like "Gee, I'm not sure," or "I'm just guessing . . ."

Five-Minute Solutions:

- Stop saying, "I don't know, but . . ." or "I'm not really sure . . ." when you really *are* sure. While speaking self-effacingly and covering up your true feelings may make men like you better and help you preserve peace in your relationships with the opposite sex, *you* pay a heavy price for constantly qualifying or hiding your true opinions in order to be liked. Hiding one's true, authentic self causes us to feel inwardly bad about ourselves—as if there's something so wrong with us no one would want to be around us if they knew who we really were/what we really thought. And self-effacing talk can *also* keep us from attaining our economic and work goals, and from having equal say and power at home, because while some men may prefer women who are tentative, they don't perceive them as very competent. Recent research (from Wellesley) indicates that men perceive a woman as *most* influential when she appears warm and friendly and competent. So, next time you're tempted to mince your words, be warm but firm and direct instead. Just think of women like Jodie Foster, Pat Schroeder, Bette Midler, and Mother Teresa—all of whom have reputations for *not* mincing words and are hugely successful in their pursuits. Then let yourself be heard.

- Give a ten-year-old a journal. Girls who keep their thoughts in journals are less likely to "forget" their true opinions, take their thoughts "underground," and lose self-assurance. Journal writing allows them to hold on to what they know and feel inside, even if, on the outside, they seem to be nodding agreeably to everyone. It helps them keep in touch with that "inner voice" they are being told to extinguish by a society that has traditionally undervalued what women have to say.

17.

Get Yourself Past the "Bad Body" Rap
●●●●●

W hen most of us look in the mirror, we're convinced our thighs aren't thin enough, our stomachs round out too much, and our breasts are either too flat, too droopy, or the wrong size. How did we grow up to be so riddled with body dislike? Raised with the media's airbrushed, flawless ideal of what female beauty ought to be (slim thighs and hips topped off by big breasts), most of us start feeling deeply unhappy about our looks as we enter adolescence and realize *our* breasts, thighs, hips, and waists aren't measuring up (or in, or out) to society's "pretty woman" standards. Isn't it time we said no to feeling bad about our bodies/ourselves if we, by nature's own design, don't meet society's deadly strict ideal of the perfect (little) woman?

Did You Know?

- In a recent survey, the majority of women said they feared getting fat more than they feared dying.
- 80% of fourth-grade girls have already been on their first diet.
- In one recent search for women with model bodies, a top modeling agency looked at 40,000 young women and found only four with bodies which met today's fashion-page standards.
- The average model weighs 23% less than the average woman.
- Today's Miss America winners weigh 15 pounds less than they did in 1954.
- If Barbie were a real woman, her measurements would be 36-18-33.

- The majority of girls in grade school say they really like themselves, but by high school, almost three in four girls no longer like themselves the way they are.
- Only 28% of adult women consider themselves attractive, while 42% of men say they feel they're handsome.
- 7 million girls and women in the U.S. suffer from eating disorders—either anorexia (self-induced starvation) or bulimia (bingeing and purging).
- Girls as young as five are now being treated for eating disorders.
- 80% of the 2 million women in America who have silicone gel breast implants—now said to be linked to a range of health problems—got them for cosmetic (not reconstructive) reasons.

Five-Minute Solutions:

- If you're a parent, take a few minutes and ask a teacher at your local high school to show the film *The Famine Within* to her or his students. This excellent, eye-opening documentary explores how young women in our culture are led to obsess about weight and body image in a way that men aren't. Both young women *and* men can benefit from seeing this—and re-seeing the way they view the female form. If you're not a parent, encourage a teen-age girl or college woman you know (or her parents) to ask a teacher or professor to check into renting this film for class. (Give her this ordering information: *The Famine Within*, Direct Cinema, 1-800-525-0000, $39.95 for individuals to purchase, $75 for institutions to rent, $195 for institutions to buy; 60- and 90-minute versions are available at the same price.) Or, if you have a friend who teaches high school or college, call and suggest this film. If you have more time, rent the film and watch it with an adolescent girl you're close to, then discuss.
- "Re-view" your body image. Did you know that most models' faces and figures are touched up and airbrushed to perfection? That even some top actresses have had body doubles do their body-baring scenes in their films? Next time you're about to let out a sigh of "I despise my thighs" or "My body is hopeless," or next time you're passing the mirror and about to chastise yourself for having hips that round out past 36 inches, catch yourself up short. Remind yourself that you're internalizing society's critical voice (it's like a tape that plays inside every woman's head) and letting it cripple your self-esteem. You're also reinforcing the way in which society values

females more for our packaging than our content. And what's more, you may be passing that message on to younger women and girls (daughters, nieces, younger sisters), who will, in turn, berate their bodies/themselves. Obviously, it's healthier to be fit than obese; but if we don't expand our definition of "fit" and stop associating fitness solely with thinness, we're simply encouraging another generation of women to grow up "dying" to be thin.

● Get one little girl you care for (a daughter, niece, or godchild) a "Happy to be me" doll. Put out by High Self-Esteem Toys (address below), this doll's rounded tummy, normal-length legs, and normal-sized waist (measurements, 36-27-38) set a more realistic ideal for girls than Barbie's anorexic 36-18-33, long-legged build. When giving this doll to a young girl, be sure you give it *in person* (since grownups, not dolls, are children's most important role models) and explain to her that *you* believe this doll is "a more realistic and healthy goal for you as you grow up." Caucasian, African American, and Asian American dolls are all available.

Resources:

To order the "Happy to be me" doll, call the 24-hour hotline: 1-800-477-9235. One doll plus one complete outfit costs $19.95 plus $3 shipping. To locate stores near you selling the doll, call: (612) 731-4767. Or write: High Self-Esteem Toys Corp., P.O. Box 25208, Woodbury, MN 55125.

The National Association of Anorexia Nervosa and Associated Disorders, Box 7, Highland Park, IL 60035, (708) 831-3438, can give you more information about these disorders.

The Renfrew Center, a full treatment and outpatient center for eating disorders, also supplies callers with information about anorexia and bulimia at (215) 482-5353; 475 Spring Lane, Philadelphia, PA 19128.

18.
Ask One College Man
to Get "Scared"
• • • • •

A number of recent studies detail the shocking frequency of rape on today's college campuses: in one study, 15 percent (more than one in seven) of college men admitted to forcing a woman to have intercourse against her will. In another report, one in twelve college males admitted to committing forceful acts that matched the *legal definition* of rape or attempted rape in order to have sex with a woman, yet only 1 percent of these men identified their behavior as rape or attempted rape. Most thought "sexual conquest" was okay (63 percent of men even said, "I get excited when a woman struggles over sex"). What can *you* do? Fortunately, new programs are springing up on college campuses to teach young men that the use of threats or force to "get" sex is not "sexual prowess" but a full-blown crime.

Did You Know?

- 1 in 4 college women have been victims of rape or attempted rape.
- 50% of college men surveyed said they would "force a woman into having sex" if they were certain they could get away with it.
- Fewer than 1 in 5 rapes on college campuses result in prosecution in criminal court.
- Only 36% of rapes on campuses result in campus penalties, and on many campuses the penalty for rape is no worse than that for plagiarism.
- Those most vulnerable to campus rape are freshman women.

- On some campuses, the weeks following the arrival of freshman women is called a fraternity's "honeymoon period" because newcomers are so naive.
- The worst offenders? Fraternities and college athletes.

Five-Minute Solutions:

- Take five minutes and ask one college man you care for (a brother, cousin, friend, or son) to do you a favor and attend a male-awareness rape program on his or a nearby campus (even if *he* doesn't need awareness training, he might share what he learns with some of his dorm buddies or frat brothers). Most campus programs are similar to SCARED (Students Concerned About Rape Education). Started at Syracuse University several years ago, this program teaches young men that force and threat-laden coercion to get sex is *rape* (not "sexual conquest"), shows them that "no" never means "maybe," and impresses upon them the trauma rape victims experience after being forced to have sex against their will. Suggest he make this your birthday, Christmas, or Chanukah present.
- Starting in September 1992, the new federal Student Right to Know and Campus Security Act goes into effect. It requires all colleges and universities which receive federal funding (even private schools receiving only a small amount of federal aid) to release information on rape statistics, facts about crime on campus, and details on campus security measures (lighting on campus, security patrolling) to any student, parent, or employee who requests them. While these facts may not yet be available in cohesive form since this law just passed, it's your legal right to push to get them. Why is requesting this information from the campus police so important? It helps combat the all too common tendency of university officials to hide or downplay occurrences of rape on campus in order to avoid bad publicity and protect the school's name.

Resources:

To Locate Men's Awareness Programs on College Campuses, contact:

1. Rus Ervin Funk, a nationwide lecturer on men's rape awareness who has listings of most campus programs and is coordinator of "Men Can Stop Rape," a program of the Men's Anti-Rape Resource Center (MARC), at P.O. Box 73559, Washington, DC 20056; (301) 386-2737.

2. Joseph Wineberg of Joseph Wineberg & Associates, an educational consultant to universities on rape prevention and resource for campus programs nationwide, 839 Williamson St. #3, Madison, WI 53703-3547; (608) 251-2821.

Security on Campus, 618 Shoemaker Rd., Gulph Mills, PA 19406; (215) 768-9330. A nonprofit, national organization that helps increase awareness about rape and crime on college campuses; lobbies for college victims' rights; offers victim assistance; and has a national database that helps college victims find legal counsel in their area. Hours of operation vary.

Campus Violence Prevention Center operates a national information clearinghouse on campus rape and violence, and sponsors the National Conference on Campus Violence. Contact Student Services, AD 108, Towson State University, Towson, MD 21204; (410) 830-2178 (Mon.–Fri., 8:30 A.M. to 4:30 P.M.).

Stop Date Rape! 23-minute color film. Student actors portray an acquaintance rape and show how it can be avoided. Three-day rental, $50. Cornell University Audiovisual Center, Media Services, 8 Research Park, Ithaca, NY 14850; (607) 255-2091.

19.

If You Are Raped, Make Sure This Rape Evidence Kit Is Used

•••••

All too often, rape victims who prosecute their attackers are *doubly* victimized—once by the rapist, and a second time by the courts as their reputations are called into question. The trial can become an ugly showdown of "her word against his," especially if there isn't enough physical evidence to prove that what took place *was* rape. But a new rape evidence collection kit, available in some hospitals and rape crisis centers, can drastically improve a victim's chances of seeing that her offender is locked away.

Did You Know?

- Only 2% to 3% of men who rape ever go to prison.
- 52% of men convicted for rape will be rearrested within three years.
- When asked, "Have you ever been the victim of rape?" one in 12 women answer yes on government surveys.
- Many women don't realize, after enduring forced sex, that what happened to them was rape. In one nationwide survey, when women were asked if they had ever experienced an incident that met the *legal definition* of rape, but in such a way that the word "rape" itself was not used ("Did X or Y ever happen to you?"), a staggering one out of four women said yes, an incident that met the legal definition of rape had happened to them.
- A new government-funded survey, which used an in-depth interview process in surveying women about rape, found that the number of rape victims is *five times* higher than previously believed.

- These new statistics represent a 59% increase in reported rape from 1989 to 1990.
- Only 16% of rape victims report their attacks to the police.
- Black women are more likely to be victims of rape than white women, yet their cases are less likely to gain media attention.

What You Can Do:

- A new evidence-gathering kit, now available in hospitals and some rape crisis centers, helps medical professionals to collect as much evidence as possible against rapists, so that later you and your lawyer stand a much better chance of convicting a rapist if you decide to prosecute. If you are ever the victim of rape—though it may be difficult in the aftermath of such a traumatizing assault—try to follow the steps below. If a friend, sister, or anyone you know ever tells you they were just raped, follow these steps with them. The more we take action to convict men who rape, the more men who rape will begin to fear the consequences of *their* actions.

1. In the aftermath of rape, dial "O" for operator and ask for the rape crisis center/rape crisis hotline near you. Often, the operator will immediately turn your call over to an operator who dispenses hotline/emergency numbers.

2. Call the rape crisis hotline, let them know you were raped, and ask them for the name of the hospital nearest you which has the "rape evidence collection kit" available. Different cities and towns have different setups: in some cities, there may be only one designated hospital which has the kit; in others, there may be a dozen or more (for instance, in Houston, there are kits in 23 area hospitals); and in yet other areas, the rape evidence collection kit is located at the rape crisis center. When you call the rape crisis hotline, they'll alert you to where it is.

The rape crisis center can also give you such advice as: Call a friend you trust and tell them what happened (having told someone can be important if you later take your case to court); don't take a shower and do not remove your clothes as they'll be needed for evidence (if you do change clothes, put them in a paper, not a plastic bag, since plastic bags gather mold and interfere with body-fluid evidence).

3. Go to the hospital or rape crisis center. Although victims often fear that if they go to the hospital, the police will automatically be called, this is not the case: the hospital is not mandated to report rape

to police. However, in some cities (e.g., Washington, DC) the police must first be notified before the rape evidence-gathering kit can be used (the police actually bring the kit to a designated hospital). Even if this is the case in your area, don't be deterred: first, you don't have to call the police yourself (the hospital can do it for you); and second, while you may have to answer some preliminary questions when the police arrive, you do not have to press charges in order to have access to the kit.

4. Don't be afraid you're going to have to go through a long, grueling procedure. When the rape evidence kit is used, the procedure is similar to a gynecologist's pelvic exam. The time the exam takes varies, depending on the extent of the assault.

The evidence, once gathered, will stay in the evidentiary freezer until *you* decide whether or not to press charges. Even if you know you *don't* want to press charges, having this exam will ensure that your medical needs have been met. If you *do* decide to press charges, following the four steps above will dramatically increase your chances of convicting the man who raped you.

Resources:

National Victim Center. For rape crisis center and hotline referrals, contact their Fort Worth office at 309 West 7th Street, Suite 705, Fort Worth, TX 76102; (817) 877-3355. They have a database of over 7000 organizations that can assist with crisis intervention, counseling, support groups, and legal counsel.

National Coalition Against Sexual Assault (NCASA), P.O. Box 21378, Washington, DC 20009; (202) 483-7165.

DC Rape Crisis Center. Call (202) 333-RAPE if you are ever raped and can't find a rape crisis center near you, to access the directory, *The Sexual Assault and Child Sexual Abuse National Directory of Victim Survivor Services and Prevention Programs*, which has a nationwide listing of rape crisis centers.

20.

Tell One Congressperson How Violence Against Women Has Harmed You
• • • • •

T he way women live: we race-walk to our cars in parking garages; watch what we wear on dates so we don't "provoke" a man to force himself on us; and worry who it might be if someone unexpectedly knocks at our door when we're alone. How can we ever get men to understand what it's like to live with this kind of ongoing, pervasive fear—and prompt male legislators on Capitol Hill to pass the pending Violence Against Women Act? Top female lobbyists suggest calling in a short, personal story of how violence against women has affected your life. Representatives often respond more to one real story from "a woman back home" than they do to foot-high stacks of anonymous-seeming petitions from people they don't know.

Did You Know?

- 61% of women (versus 32% of men) say they feel unsafe in their own neighborhoods.
- 73% of all women now over the age of twelve will be victimized, more than a third of them raped, robbed, or assaulted, at some time during their lives.
- Assaults on women ages twenty to twenty-four have jumped almost 50% in the last 15 years (compared to a 12% decrease in violence against men).
- Almost two out of three women say they watch what they wear—and choose "nonrevealing clothes"—to try to keep violent attacks from happening to them.

Phone for Action:

- Get behind the Violence Against Women Act, which would, if passed, declare rape a hate crime, giving women the same right to sue their attackers for damages that minorities have when they're the victims of crime based on bias or hatred; make funds available for more battered women's shelters; give federal grants to states to help develop violence-curbing policies such as mandatory arrest of men who physically abuse; and more. To make your voice and support of this bill heard in such a way that your representatives won't forget what you had to say when they go down to the voting floor, follow the guidelines below from top female lobbyists. (Note: if this bill has already passed by the time you read this, use these insider tips on phoning Capitol Hill to help make a difference on *any* pending bill you believe in.)

1. Get an updated "target list" naming all the representatives who are *not* yet sponsoring the Violence Against Women Act by calling NOW's Legal Defense and Education Fund (see below).

2. After getting this list, circle the name of a representative from your district or a senator from your state who isn't yet sponsoring the bill.

3. Think of a personal story—one you can relate in just four to five sentences—about how violence against women has hurt *you*, limited your life (or perhaps hurt another woman you know). If you haven't been the victim of rape or another assault, it may take a few minutes to recall a story: many of us simply don't like to think of ourselves as women who've been affected by violence. Yet when we stop to really consider whether fear of assault has limited our lives, all too often we realize how much it has. Whether it was a date who "kept going" even when you said no; a boyfriend who raised his fist at you in an argument; a time when you left the park soon after you arrived because a man started following you; or the evenings you've canceled late meetings so you could get to the car park before dark—you've probably been affected by violence. Many of us are just so used to looking over our shoulders as we go through life, we no longer notice how much fear we've come to tolerate.

4. Make the call (Senate: [202] 224-3121. House of Representatives: [202] 225-3121). If you aren't sure which congressperson represents your district, ask the main switchboard. If possible, target a

representative from your hometown, since calls from hometown folks carry extra clout (after all, you're from the place where that politician's career was launched). Or write the senator of your choice at U.S. Senate, Washington, DC 20510, or your congressperson at U.S. House of Representatives, Washington, DC 20515.

5. When you get the appropriate office, ask to speak to the legislative director (this is because your chances of getting through directly to the senator or congressperson are slim). Mention the bill by number. (Note: as of this writing, Bill S.15 in the Senate has moved out of the Senate Judiciary Committee and is now awaiting action by the full Senate. A similar measure has also been introduced by the House [Bill H.R. 1502] but has yet to come up for vote.) Now relate your story. Tell the legislative director you want your short message to be passed on *directly* to your representative. Be polite but insistent.

Finally, know this: insiders say that if as few as 15–25 women per day called a senator or representative on the target list with a real-life personal story, it would have a significant enough impact to swing that representative's vote in our direction.

Resources:

NOW Legal Defense and Education Fund, 99 Hudson Street, New York, NY 10013; (212) 925-6635. Fax: (212) 226-1066.

21.
Read This Rape Awareness List to One Man
• • • • •

Ever since the William Kennedy Smith rape trial, the media spotlight has finally been turned on date rape. Even so, most people still think of date rape as the odd, unfortunate incident. But the sad truth is that America has the highest rape rate in the world—13 times higher than England's and 20 times higher than Japan's. Rape and date rape are more common in the U.S. than left-handedness, heart attacks, or alcoholism. How do you begin to make a difference when aggression toward women—from catcalls on the street to forced sex on a date—has become so ingrained in our culture? Try reading the "Rape Awareness List for Nice Guys" below to just one nice guy (your husband or boyfriend, a male buddy, your dad, brother, or son) and ask him to spread the word among his friends. But first, ask him . . .

Does He Know?

- A woman is forcibly raped every six minutes in America.
- Based on intake made by staff at various rape counseling centers (where victims come for treatment but don't have to file police reports), 70% to 80% of women who are raped are raped by acquaintances.
- 57% of younger women who are raped are raped on a date.
- In a recent survey of Rhode Island ninth graders, *one fourth* of the boys and one sixth of the girls said that if a man spent money on a woman, he was entitled to *force* her into having sex.
- Men who initiate the date, pay all expenses, and drive are more likely to be sexually aggressive than men who don't.

- Being unable to control oneself when it comes to sex is not built into men's Y chromosome: 47% of 186 societies studied around the world are *rape-free*.
- In one study, 1 in 5 rape victims had attempted suicide and more than twice that many said they had seriously considered it.

How to Make a Difference:

- Read this "Rape Awareness List for Nice Guys" to one man you know. Ask him to always adhere to the following (yes, just for you), and to see that his friends do too. Point out that even though he probably doesn't need to hear these reminders, he might someday encounter a buddy, or know a young man, or overhear some guy in a bar, who *does*.

Rape Awareness List for Nice Guys

1. Always interrupt any buddy who you see violating—verbally or physically—a woman's space.

2. Don't join in if friends egg you on to participate in paying unwanted sexual attention to a woman at a party, in a bar, or on the street.

3. Don't ogle, whistle at, talk to, or look over women in ways that make them feel uncomfortable. If you aren't sure what makes a woman uncomfortable, ask her.

4. Never put the blame on a woman who you've heard was raped by saying things like: "She shouldn't have gone there/worn that/drank that." None of these—what she wears or drinks—excuses a crime as heinous as rape.

5. Never believe that only attractive women get raped, or imply a man wouldn't have raped a woman because "she isn't pretty." Rape is a crime of aggression, dominance, and violence. Not a beauty contest.

6. When a woman says "no," *believe* her. Never imagine "no" means "maybe" or "yes." Abandon the dangerous myth that women just can't admit they want sex and men have to overcome their hesitation. "No" means "no." Always.

7. If a woman says "maybe," but then decides "no," take no for an answer (even if you feel she's led you on, worn provocative clothes, or enjoyed being fondled). Women have the right to set limits on sexual behavior—just as you do.

8. If you feel you're getting a double message, say so. Ask her what she wants. If she says she isn't sure, assume the answer is no and let it go.

9. Never think a woman *owes* a man sex, under any circumstances. Sexual intercourse is not a payback for an expensive meal or an evening out on the town.

10. Teach sons and other young men that using force or the threat of force to coerce a date into sex is unacceptable, inappropriate, and, yes, criminal.

11. Don't confuse women's rape fantasies with how they feel about actual rape. Studies show a woman's rape fantasies (if she has them) involve romantic, loving scenarios and have nothing to do with the actual degradation and terror of being raped and physically assaulted. The two should *never* be confused.

12. Never voice, believe, or support the idea that a woman "wanted it." If you heard that a buddy who was tossed in jail for one night was raped, would you think he "wanted it"?

Resources:

Ending Men's Violence National Referral Directory helps you locate men's rape awareness groups around the country. Call the Ending Men's Violence Task Group Coordinator, Craig Norberg-Bohm, at (617) 648-5957, or write him at 50 Wyman Street, Arlington, MA 02174. Ask about their newsletter.

22.

Give a Battered Woman
This Crisis Card
• • • • •

"Why did she stay with him?" This is the question we ask when we hear that a woman who was repeatedly beaten by her husband or boyfriend has finally landed in an emergency ward. The pressures on a woman to stay with her abuser are highly complex. He may have threatened to kill her or the children if she ever tried to leave. He may have called her "ugly" and "stupid" so many times she believes him and has no willpower left to resist. Or she may simply be so confused by his hot-and-cold behavior (slapping her one minute and contritely begging her forgiveness the next) that she can no longer think clearly. Well-meaning friends and family, not knowing the extent of the danger, may even encourage her to stay, urging her to "think of the children" and offering the hope that things will get better. In short, even if she's unable to ask for it, a battered woman needs your help. So, if you know anyone who might be in trouble, take just a minute to lend her a hand. Give her the "crisis card" on p. 63.

Did You Know?

- More women are injured from battering every year than from car accidents, muggings, and stranger rapes combined.
- 20% of women's emergency room visits are for injuries inflicted during domestic violence.
- In any given year, 28% to 38% of female murder victims are killed by husbands, ex-husbands, or boyfriends.
- Super Bowl Sunday is the most violent day of the year, with the highest reported number of domestic battering cases.

- If all the women who were battered in a single year in the U.S. stood side by side holding hands, the human chain would stretch from New York City to San Francisco.

Five-Minute Solution:

- Clip out the crisis card below and carry it in your wallet. If you ever see or meet a woman you think might be battered, casually hand her the card, softening the gesture by saying simply, "I have a friend who found this helpful. Perhaps you know someone who could use it, too."

WHO TO CALL FOR HELP
IF YOU'RE A VICTIM OF DOMESTIC VIOLENCE

National Hotline: 1-800-333-SAFE

For Hearing Impaired: 1-800-873-6363

PLANNING YOUR ESCAPE:

Have the following items carefully hidden in one central place so you can grab them as you leave: bank account information, insurance policies, marriage license, a small bag with extra clothing for you and the children, phone numbers of family and friends, and an extra set of house and car keys.

Save as much of the grocery money as you can each week without arousing suspicion and squirrel it away for your escape. (Try to have about $50 in cash, including quarters for the phone.)

Think through your escape ahead of time. Know exactly *when* you'll leave, *who* you'll call, and *where* you'll go.

Resources:

Helping the Battered Woman: A Guide for Family or Friends—a small but useful pamphlet ($1) from: National Woman Abuse Prevention Center (in temporary quarters at this writing), 555 New Jersey Ave., NW, Suite 800, Washington, DC 20001; (202) 895-5271.

23.

Never Believe
"There Are No Men
Out There"
• • • • •

After the man shortage scare of the eighties, a lot of women who had long assumed they were happily single by choice suddenly panicked. Although the Harvard/Yale study that fueled the man shortage scare was quickly shown to be flawed (when the Census Bureau came out with a much more reliable study showing that 66 percent of single thirty-year-olds would wed—a number three times higher than the Harvard/Yale study), for many women the damage was done. Having been told that their matrimonial clock was ticking away, they did an overnight free fall from feeling single, secure, and satisfied to fearing they'd never marry. Even today, six years after the "Spinster Scam," some women still fear "there are no men out there." And yet . . .

Did You Know?

- Single men outnumber single women in their twenties by 2.3 million.
- Among men aged 30 to 34 there are 162 never-married men for every 100 never-married women.
- Even among 35- to 39-year-olds, there are 139 single men for every 100 single women.
- 56% of single women believe they are a lot happier than their married friends and 60% say their lives are "a lot easier."
- Only 31% of women today agree that they need a man to be "truly happy"—down from 66% in 1970.
- It is single men who, in study after study of life satisfaction, report being the least happy and having the most mental health problems of any group (single men's suicide rate is *twice* that of married men).

The Five-Second Solution:

- Stop saying, believing, and agreeing with the statement "There are no men out there." This may sound like a small way to combat the leftover fallout from the Spinster Scam, but until we change our cultural mind-set (and the attendant clichés such as this one), many women will continue to be scared into thinking, even if only in some tiny part of themselves, that there are so few men they'd better lower their standards if they want to beat the marriage odds. But if you believe that, then you *immediately* stop feeling entitled and empowered enough to ask for what you want and need in a relationship, or to say no if, for example, a man: sleeps around; throws out sexist slurs; criticizes what you eat or your weight; won't help out around the house—or in any way behaves abusively toward you.

How can you say, "No, this is unacceptable behavior," if you're scared that by doing so you'll lose the only man you think you'll ever find who (a) you're interested in, and (b) isn't already taken, engaged, or married? The answer: you can't, because you can't negotiate from a position of fear. In sum, don't accept the man shortage mythology, because lurking behind it is the message that a man who isn't good and kind to you is the best you can do. And that is *never* true.

24.
Dump Your Mommy Guilt by Doing the "Teflon Dad Test"
• • • • •

Studies show (and women know) that moms are still blamed for most of what goes wrong with the kids, from bedwetting to bad manners to tantrums in the grocery store. But today's experts say blaming it all on mom is far from fair, since genetics and a *father's* role in child rearing are paramount as well. Unfortunately, much of society (including some dads) continues to lay the responsibility and guilt at the mother's feet alone—especially if she's a working mom, and especially if the kids are in day care. Fair or not, most moms absorb that guilt all too well.

Did You Know?

- 54% of married women working full time regard child care as their responsibility, whereas only 2% of men do.
- 80% of women say that when it comes to raising the kids they feel guiltier than their husbands do.
- In one study of mental health journals, 64% of articles blamed the mother for problems in her kids like bedwetting and poor concentration—yet only about half as many articles put any blame at all on dad by saying *his* behavior affected his kids in a negative way.

Five-Minute Solutions:

- Next time you're tempted to take on a "motherlode of guilt," ask yourself, Are you letting your mate off with the Teflon treatment? First, you'll need to educate yourself about the "Big Three Myths" that mistakenly cause moms to feel overly guilt-ridden, especially when it comes to having kids in day care:

Myth 1: "Day care is bad for children's physical health because it exposes them to lots of other kids' germs." Not so, says new research from the Centers for Disease Control, which found that children who've been in day care for more than 26 months get sick at about *half* the rate of kids cared for at home (medical experts believe kids in day care may develop greater immunity to germs).

Myth 2: "Kids whose moms work feel more neglected than other kids do." While 1 in 5 children whose mothers work say they would like more time with their moms, so do an almost *equal* number of kids with stay-at-home mothers.

Myth 3: "Infants placed in day care grow up to be more anxious, needy, and neurotic than other children." Wrong again. A comprehensive new study from the Wellesley College Center for Research on Women concludes that despite many women's worries, day care infants show no signs of being more "anxious, insecure and emotionally disturbed," or unable to develop deep bonds with their moms than those kids who have stay-at-home moms.

● Now that you've helped realign your conscience, try the Teflon Dad Test. How does it work? Well, remember the test many of us used to do in college to help us see whether our dates were good guys or not? It went like this: We used to ask ourselves whether we were tolerating attitudes and behavior from the men in our lives that we would never tolerate from a female roommate. A similar test might help us to remove the "Teflon" that surrounds most dads when it comes to guilt about day care and answering our children's needs. Here's how the Teflon Dad Test works:

If you're working full time, just like your mate, next time you hear a mommy-guilting phrase from your beloved, like "How are you going to make sure that Johnny gets to soccer practice on time next week?" rather than let it play into your already well-ingrained fears about how your work life might be hurting your child/ren, ask yourself, "What am I asking of myself right now that I wouldn't ask of my husband?" As long as women singularly accept parent guilt, we'll carry a worry and burden men will never know—*or start to share.* So, say a mental no to "Teflon Daddying." Then ask your mate instead: "How can *you* help me to work out this situation?"

Resources:

If you and your husband feel overburdened with working full time and being parents, contact Parent Action, 2 Hopkins Plaza, Suite 2100, Baltimore, MD 21201 (temporary address), (410) PARENTS, an organization co-founded by Dr. T. Berry Brazelton, professor emeritus of Harvard Medical School, which studies the needs of American parents and advocates them at the community, state, and national level. Membership: $25. You'll also get their quarterly newsletter, *Parent Post*, which posts legislative alerts, and announces discounts on dozens of services.

25.
Applaud Dads Who Make Their Kids a Priority
• • • • •

More and more men today are saying, "My family is more important than my job," because they want to be around for their kids in a way that their fathers were *not* around for them. Yet many male employees say their corporate worth is still measured by whether or not they're workaholics who spend Saturdays at the office. And even when a company does offer flex time, most corporate heads frown on men who take advantage of flexible hours. Which means dads who want to put more of an emphasis on fathering need extra reassurance and applause from those around them (like us), since they aren't getting any from their bosses.

Did You Know?

- The majority of American husbands now say they would be willing to sacrifice promotions and raises at work to spend more time with their families.
- In one study, two thirds of 384 big companies did not consider it reasonable for men to take any parental leave whatsoever.
- Fewer than 3% of fathers who *are* offered unpaid parental leave by large U.S. corporations actually take it.
- Almost half of married women say they resent that their partners don't share more equally in child care duties.
- Almost two in five women cite a husband's "neglect of home or children" as a major cause of divorce—ahead of financial problems or infidelity.

Five-Minute Solutions:

- Whenever you talk to a man (a friend, colleague, brother, husband, son) who says he's thinking of cutting back on his work hours in order to take on a bigger role at home, or reconsidering a promotion because it would mean he'd have less time to spend with his kids, take a few minutes to give him verbal applause. Tell him that you think what he's doing is fantastic/the wave of the future/great daddying, and so on. The more men feel they're emotionally supported and admired if they want to put family first (which may mean a man earns less, and that could make him fear he'll be perceived by others as less powerful, influential, and desirable), the more secure they'll feel about going against their corporation's mind-set.

- If you or your husband plan to change jobs soon and you have young children, research which companies offer child care benefits and are considered family-friendly (see Section 6: Shop for a Better World for Working Moms [and Dads], as well as Section 48: Invest in Woman-Friendly Companies). If either of you faces a choice between two otherwise equally attractive opportunities, work for the company whose policies work for families.

Resources:

Give a man a copy of the report, *Men and the Work/Family Dilemma*, put out by the Families and Work Institute, 330 Seventh Avenue, New York, NY 10001; (212) 465-2044. They also operate a national clearinghouse on the effects of work on family life and the effects of families on work performance.

Catalyst, a nonprofit research organization focusing on women's (and men's) needs in business operates an Information Center, 250 Park Avenue South, New York, NY 10003-1459; (212) 777-8900, which has extensive data on paternity leave issues for fathers.

26.
Give Your Son K.P. Duty as Often as Your Daughter
• • • • •

Researchers recently found that parents hold teen-age girls far more responsible for chores—especially traditionally "female" chores like cooking, dishes, laundry, and cleaning—than they do their sons. Well-educated parents, in particular, let boys off the hook more than girls. But if parents don't raise their sons with a more enlightened sense of fairness at home, how can we expect to ever attain equality, now or in generations to come? How can we change the current fact that working women's "second shift" of household duties adds up to this: we work a full month of twenty-four hour days per year more than men do? Can we realistically hope men will *ever* fully share the burden of housework if our own sons aren't expected to?

Did You Know?

- In homes where both parents work, teen-age daughters do 10 hours of chores per week—*three times* as much as their brothers do (teen-age boys only do three hours of chores a week).
- 27% of women with teen-age children say their own lives would be better if their kids would help more with household chores.
- Kids are helping out less around the house today than they did in the past.
- If teen boys did as much housework as daughters already do, every mother in America with a teen-age son would gain an extra *fifteen* full free days this year—in other words, a two-week vacation.

Five-Minute Solutions:

- Make a chart of your children's "domestic" duties, and be sure all chores are equally distributed between the boys and the girls. You can do this quickly by drafting a list of all the household duties you regularly ask your son(s) and daughter(s) to do each week. Then ascribe a point value to each chore (say, from 1 to 3), and divide the chores among your kids (who are old enough to help out around the house) so that the points add up equally.

- Put this list on the refrigerator and tell your kids that each week, they'll each be responsible for one column of chores. The next week, they'll rotate and do the next column. When kids rotate their duties, even if one column seems slightly less attractive than another, they'll know that at the end of that week, they'll be on to a different rotation. With expectations spelled out in black and white, it won't be as likely to go unnoticed if boys aren't doing their fair share. And if today's sons aren't asked to do their fair share, what hope do we have that the problem of inequality at home will plague our daughters any less than it has us?

27.

Get Your Mammogram Done at a Reliable Lab
• • • • •

Probably no women's health issue is more hotly disputed today than the prevention of breast cancer. Even a woman's risks of getting the disease are confusing. According to the American Cancer Society, 1 in 9 women (up from 1 in 20 in 1940) will get breast cancer at some point in their lives. Others say this figure is misleading and unnecessarily frightening, since it translates to only 11% of all women getting the disease—which means 89% of us never will. How often you should get mammograms is also subject to debate. (The American Cancer Society and the National Cancer Institute recommend mammograms every other year when you're in your forties and annually after age fifty; but some doctors believe mammograms for women in their forties have no clear benefit and may actually trigger breast cancer in some susceptible women.) There's only one thing everyone seems to agree on: when you're over fifty, you should get a mammogram every year. And when you do, make sure it's done by a lab you can trust.

Did You Know?

- Studies around the world show regular mammograms cut death rates from breast cancer in women over fifty by 30% or more. In this country, this means at least 13,500 women's lives could be saved every year.
- A mammogram can detect breast tumors *two years* before a lump can be felt during a physical exam.
- In women over age fifty, mammography testing picks up existing cancer 87% of the time.

- Still, a mammogram should never be considered the last word. Some types of cancers—including 10% to 15% of all malignant lumps—don't ever show up on X-rays. And only about 10% to 12% of women under age forty whose mammograms are read as cancerous actually *have* cancer.
- Mammograms (especially those involving the dense breast tissue of young women) are notoriously hard to read. Yet 80% of U.S. radiologists have had no formal mammography training.
- Because there are no federal and few state standards for mammography equipment, the amount of radiation you're exposed to through mammograms can vary as much as *10 times* from one machine to another.
- The American College of Radiology (ACR) has a rigorous accreditation program for mammography centers. Yet as of March 1992, only 43% of the 11,000 mammography units in the U.S. had been accredited.

Five-Minute Solutions:

- Before having a mammogram, take just three minutes to call the American Cancer Society (1-800-ACS-2345) or the National Cancer Institute's Cancer Information Service Hotline (1-800-4-CANCER) to see if the center you're going to is accredited.
- Also determine whether your radiologist is board-certified by calling the American Board of Medical Specialties at 1-800-776-CERT (9 a.m. to 6 p.m. EST)
- If you're considering a lab that's not accredited (some good ones aren't because the program is voluntary), ask these five questions before making an appointment: (1) Is the equipment "dedicated"? (Dedicated machines are designed specifically for mammography and provide the best images with the least radiation.) (2) Is the person taking the mammogram a registered technologist? (To position the breast correctly and get a good image, a person should be certified by the American Registry of Radiological Technologists or licensed by the state.) (3) Is the radiologist who reads the mammograms board-certified, with special mammography training? (4) How many mammograms does the lab do? (The ACR suggests going with a facility where each radiologist reads a minimum of ten mammograms a week.) And (5) when was the machine last inspected and calibrated?

(It should be done at least once a year. If you fear you're not getting an honest answer, ask to see a copy of the inspection report.)

Resources:

To make the best decision about having a mammogram, write for the booklet *Mammogram Screening: A Decision-Making Guide,* available for $5 from the Center for Medical Consumers, 237 Thompson Street, New York, NY 10012.

The National Cancer Institute puts out a free Mammography Awareness Kit containing dozens of suggestions for raising awareness about the need for high-quality, affordable mammograms in your community. It takes only three minutes to request the kit. Simply call 1-800-4-CANCER.

28.
Sign Up for MammaCare
●●●●●

Although there has recently been controversy about the effectiveness of self breast examinations (by the time a woman can feel a lump, the cancer has often been around for years), at least 70 percent of cancerous lumps are found by women themselves, and some kinds of tumors can be caught early. So, do your monthly breast self-exams. Yet remember the limitations of this technique. If you do find a lump, don't berate yourself for not finding it sooner.

Did You Know?

- When you feel a lump, you're not actually feeling the cancer, but the "reaction" of the surrounding tissue. Some tumors create a lot of reaction, so you can feel them when the tumor is as tiny as a grain of sand. Others create no reaction until they're much larger.
- Over 80% of breast lumps are not cancerous (but they should all be checked by a physician).
- When 80 MDs from four different specialties tested their skill at finding breast lumps buried in a lifelike silicone breast model, all the doctors missed some of the lumps (15 out of 18 was the top score) and most missed more than *half* of them. (To be fair to the doctors, some of the lumps were as small as this dot ●.)
- Doctors who scored best were general internists (who had a 50% detection rate), followed by family practitioners (46%), and surgeons (42%). The lowest scorers were *gynecologists*, with a 40% success rate.

What You Can Do:

● Even though breast self-examination has limitations, you still want to try to detect breast lumps as early as you possibly can. You can learn to outperform your doctor's fingers by signing up for MammaCare, given in over 1000 hospitals, doctors' offices, and clinics around the country. In this program, you practice on the same breast model used by the 80 doctors in the study mentioned above until you learn how to detect lumps easily. With fine-tuned skill, some women learn to feel lumps the size of a pea or a small pearl.

Resources:

To find a MammaCare program in your area, dial 1-800-MAM-CARE or write MammaCare, P.O. Box 15748, Gainesville, FL 32604. If you're too strapped for time to attend a class (or there's no program in your area), you and a few friends may want to band together to buy an at-home kit ($74, shipping included), which contains a silicon breast model plus instruction booklets and a videocassette to guide you.

National Alliance of Breast Cancer Organizations, 2nd Floor, 1180 Avenue of the Americas, New York, NY 10036, (212) 719-0154 or (212) 221-3300, has a wealth of educational resources, including their quarterly newsletter *NABCO News*.

29.
Pregnant?
Check Your Doctor's
C/NB Score
• • • • •

Cesarian delivery is now the most frequently performed major operation in the U.S., costing American parents $3 billion a year. There's no doubt that when a woman has a complicated pregnancy or delivery, birth by Cesarian section can save her or her baby's life. Yet most women—including about 80% of those who previously delivered by C-section—are capable of giving birth vaginally. So before hiring an ob/gyn, check his or her C/NB score (percentage of Cesarians to natural births).

Did You Know?

● Between 1965 and 1987, birth by Cesarian section in this country skyrocketed over 400%.

● The National Center for Health Statistics has predicted that if current trends continue, 40% of births could be done by Cesarian by the year 2000.

● According to a report from the Public Citizen Health Research Group, an estimated half of the nearly 1 million Cesarians performed in the U.S. each year are unnecessary.

● The U.S. has the highest Cesarian rate in the world.

● A Cesarian adds an average of 66% to the cost of having a baby. In 1989 (the latest year for which figures are available), the cost of a normal pregnancy and delivery in the U.S. averaged $4334, whereas Cesarian section cost an average of $7186.

● If your delivery is covered by insurance, you're twice as likely to have a C-section as a woman without insurance.

Five-Minute Solutions:

- Think of yourself as an employer, not a patient. You're hiring a doctor, and you need to know his/her credentials. Make sure you ask these questions: What is your Cesarian rate? (A doctor with many high-risk patients may justifiably have a C-section rate as high as 17%. But for most doctors, a rate higher than 10% to 12% is a red flag. If your doctor's score is higher than that, ask whether a large proportion of his patients are high risk.) Also ask: Under what circumstances will you perform a C-section? What can I do to avoid these situations? What support can I expect from you to keep from having a Cesarian? If any answer makes you uneasy, find a doctor you're more comfortable with.

- Also choose your birth place with care. If a hospital has a high Cesarian rate, you put yourself at high risk of surgery. A hospital's Cesarian rate is public information you have a right to know. If the hospital absolutely refuses to release this figure, you may be able to find it in the paperback *Women's Health Alert,* by Sidney M. Wolfe, MD, which lists C-section rates at 2453 U.S. hospitals. Or order *Unnecessary Cesarean Sections: Halting A National Epidemic* by Ingrid Van Tuinen and Sidney M. Wolfe, MD, ($10.00) from The Public Citizen Health Research Group, 2000 P Street NW, Suite 700, Department CS, Washington, DC 20036, (202) 833-3000.

- Investigate the possibility of having your baby in a certified nurse-midwife—run birthing center. Based on the idea that birth should be a joyous family affair, birthing centers offer a number of advantages: lower cost (an average of up to 50% less than regular hospital stays); shorter stays after birth; and lower Cesarian rates (4.4% in birth centers compared to an overall average of more than 23% in hospitals). Studies consistently show birthing centers are as safe (or safer) than hospitals. But a certified center always has an arrangement with a nearby hospital so in those few cases when problems do develop, a woman can be transferred to a hospital in a matter of minutes.

- Urge your state legislators to pass the Maternity Information Act (already passed in New York and Massachusetts), which requires hospitals to release information to women when they register about how many Cesarians they perform. Similar acts are pending in California, Pennsylvania, Texas, and New Mexico. (Contact I-CAN below for more information.)

- To help other women avoid surgery, order the poster "Things You Can Do to Avoid an Unnecessary Cesarian" ($3 from I-CAN), and ask a nurse or doctor you know to hang it where a lot of pregnant women will see it.

Resources:

International Cesarian Awareness Network (I-CAN), P.O. Box 152, Syracuse, NY 13210; (315) 424-1942. Has a wealth of information, including the $3 poster mentioned above, scientific studies from such prestigious journals as the *New England Journal of Medicine,* and a free reading list of "Sources for Discovering the Ways and Wisdom of Birth."

National Association of Childbearing Centers, 3123 Gottschall Road, Perkiomenville, PA 18074; (215) 234-8068. Send $1 for a list of centers or midwives in your area.

National Association of Childbirth Assistants, 205 Copco Lane, San Jose, CA 95123, (408) 225-9167, can put you in touch with a certified childbirth assistant in your area.

30.

Before a Hysterectomy, Call HERS
•••••

"Y ou need a hysterectomy." At current hysterectomy rates, one in three American women reading this sentence will hear those four words from her doctor before she turns sixty. Some hysterectomies (those to treat uterine cancer, for example) are unquestionably necessary. But nearly 90% of these operations are performed to "cure" benign diseases—such as fibroids or ovarian cysts—which can often be treated with less radical surgery or no surgery at all. So, if your doctor utters these four frightening words, don't sign those consent forms until you get all the facts. (As you read the following, keep in mind that many women who've had hysterectomies report no problems whatsoever, which emphasizes that whether or not to have this operation is a highly personal decision every woman must make for herself.)

Did You Know?

- Hysterectomy is the second most common major surgery in this country (the most common is birth by Cesarian section).
- While half of all women who have hysterectomies don't suffer complications, half *do*—and every year 1 in 1,000 patients (or 600 women) die due to complications following the operation.
- Your risks of having a hysterectomy depend partly on where you live. Southern states have the highest rates, Northeastern states the lowest.
- After having hysterectomies, 33% to 46% of women in one study had difficulty becoming sexually aroused or reaching orgasm.

- Premenopausal women face nearly triple the risk of heart disease after hysterectomy—even if their ovaries aren't removed (some doctors suspect the uterine hormone prostacyclin guards young women against heart problems).
- If hysterectomy rates were as low in the U.S. as in Denmark and the United Kingdom, American gynecologists would collectively lose at least $1.05 billion annually. That's an income loss of $32,530 a year for each ob/gyn in the U.S.

What You Can Do:

- Before having a hysterectomy for a nonlife-threatening condition, take just five minutes to write or call the HERS (Hysterectomy Educational Resources and Services) Foundation, 422 Bryn Mawr Avenue, Bala Cynwyd, PA 19004; (215) 667-7757. Know before you call that this organization's founder, Nora Coffey, is anti-hysterectomy (her life was changed forever by the operation). But she has a wealth of information, including a short referral list of doctors skilled at performing less radical surgeries.
- If you know any woman considering a hysterectomy, photocopy this page and give it to her.

More Resources:

The National Women's Health Network, 1325 G Street NW, Washington, DC 20005, (202) 347-1140, has an excellent packet of information presenting all sides of the hysterectomy controversy for $5. They also have individual packets ($5 each) on many disorders for which hysterectomies are commonly recommended, including endometriosis, fibroids, ovarian cysts, and pelvic inflammatory disease.

31.
Confront the
New Sexual Reality
• • • • •

Are you a smart woman "acting dumb" about AIDS? If so, you're not alone. In one recent Pennsylvania study, 72% of women have never used condoms during casual sex, whereas 67% never used them with their regular partner. (Many women say they don't know how to bring up the subject without hurting a man's feelings.) Unfortunately, being too considerate of a lover's ego nowadays can literally kill you. So, if you're uneasy about insisting that a man put on a condom, you may just want to wear one yourself.

Did You Know?

- Women are the fastest-growing group of AIDS patients. Between 1989 and 1990, reported AIDS cases in women rose 34%, compared with a 22% increase in men.
- The World Health Organization predicts that by the year 2000 as many as 80% of AIDS cases will be transmitted heterosexually.
- A healthy woman who has sex with an infected man is 14 times more likely to contract the AIDS virus than a healthy man who sleeps with an infected woman.
- In New York City, AIDS is already the number-one cause of death in women between ages 25 and 34.
- Women are excluded from most clinical trials of AIDS drugs. Result: Treatments that prolong men's lives may *harm* women. Lab studies of the widely used drug AZT, for example, reveal the side effect in female mice of vaginal cancer.

What You Can Do:

● Don't put a man's ego above your own life. If your lover refuses to wear a condom, take charge of your own health by keeping a stock of female condoms on hand and wearing one every time you make love. One female condom—a polyurethane sheath aptly marketed under the brand name "Reality"—has two diaphragmlike rings: one fits over the cervix, the other hangs outside, rimming the vagina. It should be available in drugstores for about $2.25 by the end of the year. The other, the Bikini Condom, is a latex panty that covers the genital area and has a built-in pouch that's pushed into the vagina before intercourse. Some women protest that the female condom is just another way to put the whole burden of sexual responsibility on women—and they have an excellent point. But until men do take on more responsibility for safe sex, don't let political correctness be your top priority when we're talking about saving your life.

Resources:

One of the best resources on the topic is the $5 AIDS packet put out by the National Women's Health Network, 1325 G Street NW, Washington, DC 20005; (202) 347-1140. They have just compiled a list of reputable women-owned or women-run clinics throughout the country. Call for a referral.

Kathleen Stoll, senior associate at the National Resource Center on Women and AIDS at the Center for Women Policy Studies, 2000 P. Street NW, Suite 508, Washington, DC, 20036, (202) 872-1770, can answer any questions you might have about legislation affecting women and AIDS.

AIDS: Women at Risk, a $1 pamphlet available from: The National Consumers League, 815 15th Street NW, Suite 928, Washington, DC 20005, (202) 639-8140.

32.

Give This List to One Pregnant Teen

• • • • •

W hen she discovers she's pregnant, a teenager has usually never felt more terrified and alone. She doesn't need to be told she made a mistake (she already knows that). What she most needs at this frightening time is someone to understand and support her as she makes what may well be the toughest decision of her life. So, if you know a pregnant teen, let her know she's not alone. Give her this list of resources to help her make the right choice—for her.

Did You Know?

- Every year in the U.S. more than 1 million teens become pregnant. 125,000 of them are age fifteen or younger.
- U.S. teen pregnancy rates are among the highest in all industrial nations—twice as high as England and Wales, Canada and France, three times higher than Sweden, and seven times higher than the Netherlands.
- 50% of pregnant teens decide to have and keep the baby, 40% choose abortion, and about 10% opt for adoption.
- Before having an abortion, a minor currently has to obtain one or both parents' consent in 18 states (as of this writing). See p. 96 for listing.

What You Can Do:

- One of the best resources for helping a teen make the best choice for her is the pamphlet *Unsure About Your Pregnancy? A Guide to*

Making the Right Decision for You, put out by the National Abortion Federation (1436 U Street NW, Suite 103, Washington, DC 20009; [202] 667-5881). This well-designed guide doesn't push a girl to have an abortion. Rather, it gives her many insightful questions to ponder ("What are the two or three things I hope to have or achieve in the next five or ten years? How would having a baby help? How would adoption help? How would abortion help?"), then leaves the decision entirely to her. Just order this pamphlet for 50 cents and give it to a girl you want to help.

- For pregnancy tests, nonpreachy pregnancy counseling, and contraceptives to prevent future pregnancies, direct a girl to the Planned Parenthood clinic closest to her (ask the operator for the local number or call 1-800-555-1212 for the nearest 1-800 Planned Parenthood number).

- If a girl is considering abortion, be sure to give her the section on avoiding bogus abortion clinics on p. 99.

Resources for Preventing Teen Pregnancy:

The Adolescent Pregnancy Prevention Clearinghouse at the Children's Defense Fund (25 E Street NW, Washington, DC 20001; 202-628-8787) has a $1 brochure entitled *Preventing Children Having Children: What You Can Do.* They also offer "adolescent pregnancy prevention" posters. One simply shows a large pregnant tummy under the caption: IF YOU'RE EMBARRASSED BY A PIMPLE, TRY EXPLAINING THIS ($4). Ask your junior high or high school principal to hang one in the girls' locker room.

33.

Give One Teen Girl an "Information Vaccine" Against AIDS

●●●●●

T eens have many misconceptions about AIDS: "You can't get it from a nice guy"; "After you've slept with a boy several times, you don't need a condom anymore"; and even, "It can't happen to me." If every woman in this country took just five minutes during the next month to give one teen-age girl the real facts about AIDS, by the end of the month there wouldn't be a teen-age girl left in America who hadn't been given an "information vaccine."

Does She Know?

- Statistics on how many teens are infected with the HIV virus are hard to come by. But one recent study suggests the rate of infection among teens may be 10 times higher than researchers previously thought.
- Between 1985 and 1988 alone, the death rate for women from AIDS quadrupled. In 1991, AIDS was one of the five leading causes of death in young women, ages thirteen to thirty-nine.
- Since it may take 10 years or longer after being infected to get AIDS, there are far more cases of infection among teens than are being reported. About one in four women with AIDS is in her twenties and was probably infected in her teens.
- The golden rule for preventing AIDS among teens is simple and can be shared in a minute: Don't have sex; but if you ever do have sex, always use a latex condom with a spermicide (spermicides can kill sexually transmittable germs if a condom breaks or leaks). If you use a lubricant, use a water-based one, since oil-based lubricants can leave condoms vulnerable to breakage.

- Many girls feel reassured when a boy talks openly about AIDS, as if his willingness to discuss the matter means he's somehow "safe." But one study found that males who talk about AIDS (but who rarely or never use condoms) have nearly 50% more partners than those who clam up and won't talk.
- According to a study reported in the *New England Journal of Medicine*, 20% of men (but only 4% of women) say they would lie to a date about having had a negative HIV-antibody test in order to get sex.

What You Can Do:

- Photocopy this page and give it to just one teen girl (or her mother). You might also want to give her a copy of the book *Risky Times: How to Be AIDS-Smart and Stay Healthy*, by Jeanne Blake ($5.95 by phoning Workman Publishing Company at 1-800-722-7202). The book comes with a handy parents' guide to help you broach the subject with your own daughter, niece, or granddaughter.

Resources:

"101 Ways to Make Love Without Doin' It," a folder for young teens, which you could pass out at a girls' club meeting or even to an entire junior high class. It's available in bulk ($15 for 50 copies) from ETR Associations/Network Publications at 1-800-321-4407.

Teens Teaching Teens AIDS Prevention (TEENS TAP), 1-800-234-TEEN (Mon.–Fri., 4:00 P.M. to 8:00 P.M. CT), a national toll-free AIDS hotline run for teenagers by teenagers, where a girl (or boy) can feel safe asking such confidential questions as "How can I tell if I have AIDS?" and "If I'm going to have sex, how can I protect myself?"

34.
Don't Be a Woman in Waiting
• • • • •

Women's bathrooms may seem like a silly "health" topic. Yet any woman who's ever been to the theater, opera, concert, or sports coliseum knows just how frustrating it can be to stand in a long line outside the ladies' room (as men march merrily in and out of the men's room) when the "back to your seats" bell sounds. At that moment, it's a quick choice between missing the first scene of the second act, or watching it with our legs tightly crossed (particularly problematic if you suffer from urinary tract infections). Tired of standing politely in line? Enter "potty politics" . . .

Did You Know?

- Public men's rooms have more facilities than women's rooms do. (In New York, before passage of new requirements, public buildings had seven stalls/urinals in the men's room—and only three stalls in the ladies' room).
- A recent study found women require nearly twice as much time to use the toilet as men—80 seconds vs. 45 seconds.
- And we don't take longer because we're powdering our noses: we have to deal with more restrictive clothing than men (such as pantyhose and jumpsuits); we're the ones who get pregnant and need restrooms more frequently; and we're the ones who take young children in the ladies' room with us (particularly at places like the zoo or amusement park), which makes it even more crowded.

Five-Minute Solutions:

- If this issue has you upset, check out the status of "potty parity" laws in your state. Some legislators have instituted state laws requiring that all new or remodeled public buildings have as many (or more) toilets in women's restrooms as there are in the men's. So far, potty parity laws have passed in 10 states—California, Florida, Illinois, Maryland, Michigan, New York, North Carolina, Pennsylvania, Texas, and Wisconsin.

- If your state isn't active on potty parity, find a local female legislator and ask her to suggest this law. If the legislation is already pending, write and call your legislators so this issue will be taken seriously (for help in finding your legislators, see Section 40: Get Ready to Fight for *Roe* in Your Backyard, p. 101).

- There's even an expert you can direct your legislator to if she wants to draft a law from scratch. One of the nation's best experts on this topic is Kathie Kidder Jones—CEO of Urinette, (904) 944-9779, 7012 Pine Forest Rd., Pensacola, FL 32526. Jones knows all the intricate details about writing a law that works. (For example, says Jones, some legislators haven't written it into their laws that their state bill supersedes inequitable local building codes—which means the new state law may not have any real effect.)

35.
Earmark Your Funds for Women's Concerns
•••••

When you see on the nightly news that another prenatal clinic or battered women's shelter has had to close for lack of funding, or hear that there isn't sufficient money being spent on breast cancer research, you may cry, "Why doesn't somebody do something?" Fortunately, you can. The next time you're asked to give at the office, if the donations are going to United Way, simply take one minute to make sure the money you give goes to a women's program you deeply believe in. If, in the wake of recent controversy surrounding United Way, your corporation is looking for a new fundraising group, take this opportunity to encourage them toward more woman-friendly fundraising organizations.

Did You Know?

- Less than 5% of the philanthropic dollars in a 1990 sample of foundation grants went to programs directly benefiting women and girls.
- Depending on the foundation, 65% to 100% of funds for girls' and women's programs comes from women.
- 71% of foundation board members are men.
- Many professional fundraisers say having "women" or "girls" in the name of an organization or program has become the "kiss of death" to successful fundraising.
- Even United Way consistently gives more to men and boys than to women and girls. In 1990, United Way gave the YMCA $39 million more than it gave the YWCA and the Boy Scouts $32 million more than the Girl Scouts.

Five-Minute Solutions:

- While no woman alone can solve the problem that women's concerns are so much less funded than men's, together we can make a huge difference. If every woman in the U.S. gave only $5 a month to programs benefiting women and children, we'd put $5.6 billion a year to work for women and girls—more than the gross national product of Bolivia.

- If you give to United Way, make sure your dollars go where you want them to. Find a worthy program in your area—perhaps a battered women's shelter, or a hospital doing breast cancer research. Check with the person in charge of collections in your office to make sure the program you want to fund meets United Way "criteria." Then simply write the project name on the "designated agency" line of your donor card. Better yet, give directly to your chosen program.

- If you want to support a specific cause (such as a local rape crisis center or women's sports program) but have no idea where to begin, contact: National Network of Women's Funds, 1821 University Avenue, Suite 409N, St. Paul, MN 55104; (612) 641-0742. The women here can help you find a cause you truly believe in. They also have a 21-minute video (perfect for showing at a women's club meeting) called *Why Women's Funds?* ($25).

- Encourage your office to look into organizations that do workplace fundraising for such causes as saving the environment and helping women and minorities. Contact the National Committee for Responsive Philanthropy, 2001 S Street NW, #620, Washington, DC 20009; (202) 387-9177.

Resources:

Resourceful Women, 3543 18th Street, San Francisco, CA 94110; (415) 431-5677. This network helps women who've inherited $25,000 or more learn how to manage their wealth. Their handy pocket guide, *Make Change Happen* ($1 with a large self-addressed envelope stamped with 45 cents postage), lists 100 foundations set up to make the world better for women and everyone else.

36.

Use Your Voice for Choice

•••••

When the Supreme Court ruled in 1973 in *Roe* v. *Wade* that the Constitution protects a woman's right to choose, many women understandably believed the abortion battle was won. Unfortunately, the real battle has just begun. Even though one poll found 73% of Americans support a woman's right to choose, anti-abortion groups are well financed and highly effective: they're cutting off funds to abortion providers on every front. What can you do in the face of this overwhelming turn of the tide against women's rights? Start by choosing a phone company that supports choice. Every time you make a long-distance call, you'll put a few cents in the pro-choice coffers—and it won't cost you an extra dime.

Did You Know?

- Federal funding for abortions is already gone, and private funding is rapidly drying up.
- In 1988, United Way stopped funding Planned Parenthood.
- In 1990, after a fierce letter-writing campaign and under threat of boycott from anti-abortionists, AT&T cut off its contributions to Planned Parenthood after 25 years of support.
- Ironically, the money AT&T once gave Planned Parenthood wasn't even used for abortions. For years, at AT&T's request, the funds had been used exclusively for teen pregnancy prevention programs.

Five-Minute Solutions:

- "When you donate money to United Way, specify how much of it you want to go to Planned Parenthood. (Though United Way doesn't fund PP directly, they will pass the money along.)

- Although AT&T has a good reputation when it comes to recruiting women and providing child care, how good can any company be for women if they don't support choice? So switch from AT&T to Sprint or MCI and write AT&T chairman of the board Robert E. Allen (AT&T, 32 Avenue of the Americas, New York, NY 10013, or call [212] 605-5500) to tell him why.

- Better yet, sign up with Working Assets Long Distance (1-800-788-8588). Not only are their rates as cheap or cheaper than the three other major telephone carriers, but 1% of every call you make goes into an action fund, which is divvied up at the end of the year among a variety of environmental, peace, and human rights groups. Women's organizations funded by the program typically include Planned Parenthood, the National Abortion Rights Action League (NARAL), the National Black Women's Health Project, and the National Network of Women's Funds.

  When you sign up with Working Assets, each phone bill comes with a description of upcoming legislation of interest. By taking just two seconds to check a box when you pay your bill, you can have a pre-written Citizen Letter ($3) sent to a legislator in your name stating your views about the issue of the month. And on the first Monday of every month, Working Assets also allows you to make four three-minute calls to Congress for free.

- Still a third (and perhaps the best) way to support choice with your phone dollars: call your local NARAL (get the number by calling NARAL's National Office at [202] 408-4600) to see if they have a "Use Your Voice for Choice" program. These programs are just getting started, so you may have to shop around for one. But in Maryland, for example, if you sign up for the Affinity Fund, a whopping 8% of your phone bill every time you make a long-distance call within the U.S. goes to Maryland NARAL. (Contact them at 817 Silver Spring Ave., Suite 409, Silver Spring, MD 20910, [301] 565-4154, for details.) Rates at the time of writing were actually lower than AT&T's.

37.
Wear a Bracelet
for Becky
• • • • •

Laws requiring a pregnant teen to involve one or both parents or a judge before having an abortion often sound reasonable: if your daughter were pregnant, wouldn't you want to know so you could help her through such a difficult time? Unfortunately, there are some little-known facts about parental consent laws that may make you want to fight to keep them from being enacted (or get them repealed) in your state.

Did You Know?

- Even when laws don't require it, most pregnant teens discuss abortion with their parents before having one.
- A fifteen- to nineteen-year-old girl is *twenty-four times* more likely to die from childbirth than from a legal first-trimester abortion.
- Young women who don't or can't tell their parents may have compelling reasons. In the book *Backlash,* Susan Faludi tells the story of Spring Adams, a thirteen-year-old Idaho girl on welfare who was raped and impregnated by her father in 1989. After a frantic search, her mother finally located an Oregon clinic that agreed to give Spring an abortion for $200 (the most she could afford). Tragically, two days before the girl was to board the Greyhound bus to Portland, her father—who adamantly opposed abortion—shot her to death with an assault rifle.
- 17 of the 18 states requiring parental consent (as of this writing) also have "judicial bypass laws," which allow a young woman reluctant to tell her parents to get permission for an abortion from a judge.

Unfortunately, such laws often work better in theory than practice. After discovering she was pregnant in 1988, seventeen-year-old Becky Bell of Indianapolis, Indiana, went before a judge and was denied a legal abortion. After telling a friend she loved her parents so much she couldn't bear to disappoint them, Becky sought an illegal abortion instead. Complications from the back-alley operation killed her. Her parents have since gone on a nationwide campaign in the hopes of getting parental consent laws repealed.

What You Can Do:

- If parental consent laws disturb you, wear a memorial bracelet for Becky Bell until these laws are repealed. When anyone asks you about the bracelet, take just a minute to tell them Becky's story. The bracelet ($11 in brass or nickel silver, $33 in sterling silver) is available from: The Fund for the Feminist Majority, 8105 W. 3rd Street, #1, Los Angeles, CA 90048; (213) 651-0495; or 1600 Wilson Blvd, #704, Arlington, VA 22209; (703) 522-2214.
- At this writing, 18 states had mandatory parental notice or consent laws: AL, AR, CT, IN, LA, MA, ME, MI, MN, MO, ND, OH, RI, SC, UT, WV, WI, WY. To fight parental consent laws in your state, see the primer for making grass-roots change under Section 40: Get Ready to Fight for *Roe* in Your Backyard, p. 101.

Resources:

The Alan Guttmacher Institute, 111 Fifth Avenue, New York, NY 10003; (212) 254-9891. Their free one-page "Facts in Brief: Abortion in the U.S." will give you dozens of facts at your fingertips so you'll sound like you've done your homework when you call or write your local legislator about this issue.

Another useful fact sheet is "Teenage Women, Abortion, and the Law," free from the National Abortion Federation, 1436 U Street NW, Suite 103, Washington, DC 20009; (202) 667-5881.

38.
Pledge a Picket
· · · · ·

W hile the number of abortion clinics is rapidly decreasing, the number of anti-choice demonstrators is on a dramatic rise. These picketers have been known to injure people so regularly that in some areas, clients have been escorted into the clinic (for their protection) in a four-sided plywood box, with no top or bottom and carrying handles on the sides. In what has been reported as "mob brutality," anti-abortion protesters have already hit more than 683 clinics. What can you do? Pledge a few cents per picketer. Read on to find out how.

Did You Know?

- Anti-abortionists picketed clinics 275 times in 1991, up from 45 times in 1990.
- In 1991, arsonists alone did $1,055,000 in damage to abortion clinics: between 1977 and 1991, clinics were torched or bombed 94 times, vandalized 309 times, and terrorized with 262 bomb threats.
- In 80 incidents so far, clinic staff members have received death threats, and in 71 cases, they've been physically beaten, taken hostage, or hit by protesters' cars.
- Anti-abortion arsonists maimed one doctor when they booby-trapped her morning newspaper.

Five-Minute Solutions:

- A growing number of Planned Parenthood clinics now have "Pledge a Picket" programs. Whenever anti-abortionists picket a clinic, you agree to donate a sum (say 25 cents) for every picketer who shows up. The more numerous picketers become, the more money the pro-choice side gets—and the picketers know it. For more information, contact the Planned Parenthood clinic in your area.

- To tell your U.S. senator or representative you oppose the "gag ruling," which keeps nurses and counselors in clinics from even mentioning the abortion option to patients, call Western Union (1-800-325-6000) and dictate a Public Opinion Message ($9.95 for 20 words or less, $3.50 for each additional 20 words). The telegram will be sent to the White House or Capitol Hill in a matter of hours. (Western Union has one of those irritating phone lines answered by a machine; to save time, don't push any buttons on your touchtone phone: just hold until a real person answers.) This strategy works best when used a day or two before an important vote is coming up in the House or Senate.

Resources:

Planned Parenthood Federation of America, 810 7th Avenue, New York, NY 10019; (212) 541-7800. If you can't find a Planned Parenthood in your local phone directory, phone this number to find a clinic near you.

39.

Avoid Phony Abortion Clinics
• • • • •

Abortion clinics are far more difficult to find nowadays because there are much fewer of them. What's worse, once you find one, it may secretly be run by anti-abortionists who use scare tactics to frighten women away from having an abortion and try to browbeat them into having unwanted children. If you're considering an abortion, do your research first—and call the hotline listed below. If women stop getting lured into these phony clinics, they won't stay around long.

Did You Know?

- Over 2000 clinics in the U.S. that advertise in the Yellow Pages and look like legitimate abortion clinics are, in fact, run by anti-abortionists who dress like nurses and trick a woman into thinking she's in a real clinic, then traumatize her by describing abortion in (falsely) grisly detail.
- These fake clinics lure in over 600,000 unsuspecting women a year.
- They coax women in over the phone by using step-by-step guidelines provided to them by the anti-choice group Operation Rescue. These instructions include, "When a woman calls, be vague . . . don't answer her questions . . . tell her that you'll answer all of her questions after she arrives."
- Since 1977 (due to vigorous anti-abortion lobbying), the number of legitimate abortion clinics has decreased dramatically. Today, only 17% of the 3135 counties in the United States provide abortion services.

- In rural areas, a staggering 93% of rural counties have no abortion services.
- In 1985, 23% of training hospitals with programs in obstetrics-gynecology required their medical residents to learn how to perform abortions, but today less than 12% of such institutions now require training for abortions.

Five-Minute Solutions:

- For a referral to a legitimate clinic near you, call the National Abortion Federation referral line: 1-800-772-9100 (Mon.–Fri., 9:30 A.M. to 5:30 P.M. ET). If it's an emergency and you can't get through on the hotline (which is often very busy), you can call NAF's regular business number (listed below).
- If you're searching for a clinic on your own because the above hotline has no referral in your area, rather than choosing a clinic from the Yellow Pages, call your local or state medical society or hospital and ask for a referral from them.
- Once you've found a clinic, double-check its legitimacy by asking pointed questions: How many doctors are on staff? What is the doctor's name and experience? How many abortions do they perform a year? When you get vague or evasive answers, be suspicious.
- Many anti-abortion clinics are set up beside real clinics to confuse you—they hope you'll walk in their door by mistake, on your way to the real clinic. When going into a clinic, be sure to check the name and address before walking inside.

Resources:

National Abortion Federation, 1436 U Street NW, Suite 103, Washington, DC 20009; (202) 667-5881. Write for their excellent information packet containing abortion fact sheets and the pamphlet *Having an Abortion: Your Guide to Good Care*. Pamphlet available in English and Spanish (50 cents).

40.
Get Ready to Fight for *Roe* in Your Backyard

•••••

How close are you to losing your right to choose an abortion? That depends on which state you're in. The National Abortion Rights Action League (NARAL) recently predicted that if *Roe* v. *Wade* was weakened by the Supreme Court, which it was in June 1992 when the Court gave states sweeping new power to restrict abortion without outlawing it, fifteen million women in thirteen states will probably find their right to a legal abortion greatly restricted. Although Democrats, as of this writing, planned to introduce the Freedom of Choice Act (a bill that would ensure a woman's right to choose by writing *Roe* v. *Wade* into federal law), most analysts agree that even if this bill did pass Congress, it would never be able to withstand a Bush veto. If analysts are right, there's only one way to protect your freedom of choice: by getting your state legislature to pass its own pro-choice law.

Did You Know?

If our government no longer protects a woman's right to choose a safe and legal abortion, how bad it can get in various states? Here are a few examples. (At this writing, none of these laws was yet in effect because all were tied up in court battles.)

- Under a Pennsylvania law (which has now been upheld by the Supreme Court), a twenty-four-hour waiting period after counseling has been imposed on a woman.
- In 1991, Utah passed a law under which a woman who had an abortion could be prosecuted for murder and, if found guilty, shot by

a firing squad. After a public outcry, Utah lawmakers added a "clari-
fying" amendment to ensure no one convicted under the law would
be shot. But a woman or doctor participating in an illegal abortion (an
abortion that's performed for purposes other than saving a pregnant
woman's life, in cases of rape or incest, or in a few other narrow
circumstances) can still be tried for murder in Utah.

● Louisiana recently passed a law making abortion legal only in cases
of rape, incest, or to save the mother's life. Doctors providing other
abortions would be sentenced to up to 10 years of hard labor.

What You Can Do:

Even states like California (where a woman's right to choose an abortion
seems fairly well protected) often have only a slim pro-choice majority
in the state legislature. So, no matter where you live, it's important to
know what your lawmakers are up to (a lot simpler than it might sound).
You can easily do the four simple steps below in one hour. Once you
know how to reach your state representatives and keep up to date on
abortion laws being voted on, it will take only 5 minutes a month to keep
the pressure on. Here's a primer for making state-by-state grass-roots
change. (You can also adapt these steps and use them to fight for other
issues you care deeply about.)

1. Call your city town hall (ask the operator for the number if you
can't find it). Then call your local Board of Elections at town hall, and
ask who your state representatives are. Get their phone numbers and
addresses.

2. Call the National Abortion Rights Action League at (202) 408-
4600 to get the number of your state NARAL office. Then make a
second call to your state NARAL to find out your legislators' stance on
abortion (and other women's issues). If NARAL has no office in your
state, call the National Organization for Women ([202] 331-0066) and
get the number of your state NOW, instead.

3. Share everything you find out with at least two friends.

4. Write a brief note telling your local legislators how you feel about
their stands on abortion. Tell a personal story illustrating why you feel
as you do.

5. Once you know where your local politicians stand, vote for pro-
choice candidates in every election. Urge your friends to do the same.

Resources:

National Abortion Rights Action League, 1101 14th Street NW, Washington, DC 20005, (202) 408-4600, the place to contact for the very latest information on the status of your right to choose. Subscribe to the *NARAL News* ($25 a year), or ask for their *State by State Review of Abortion Rights* ($10).

National Council of Jewish Women, 53 West 23rd Street, New York, NY 10010; (212) 645-4048. This nearly 100-year-old organization has been active in reproductive rights since the 1920s, when they worked with Margaret Sanger (the birth control pioneer). To get involved in their pro-choice movement on a state level, look up your local NCJW branch in the phone directory, or call their New York office to find the number of the NCJW nearest you.

Catholics for a Free Choice, 1436 U Street NW, Suite 301, Washington, DC 20009, (202) 986-6093, has an excellent quarterly newsletter called *Conscience* ($10), which keeps you up to date on the latest abortion issues.

Republicans for Choice, 1315 Duke Street, Suite 201, Alexandria, VA 22314; (703) 836-8907. Worked vigorously to change the anti-choice position in the Republican party platform at the 1992 National Convention and at last report was gearing up to fight for choice on a state-by-state level.

American Women at Risk: The Threat to Legal Abortion

If <u>Roe</u> v. <u>Wade</u> is overturned or eviscerated, here are the states where a woman's right to choose will be at risk, based on an analysis of the positions of governors and state legislators.

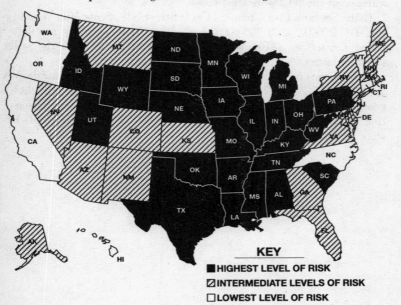

KEY

- ■ HIGHEST LEVEL OF RISK
- ▨ INTERMEDIATE LEVELS OF RISK
- □ LOWEST LEVEL OF RISK

XII. Political Power

41.
Always Check "Ms."
• • • • •

Some politicians are now beginning to put together computerized lists of women who check "Ms." on their voter registration cards. Why? Because they're convinced that, compared to women who use "Miss" or "Mrs.," women who call themselves "Ms." care more deeply about such issues as the right to choose abortion, family leave, day care, and violence against women. A few market researchers are starting to select Ms. lists, too. So, whenever you fill out a standard form—whether it's a voter registration card or a consumer product satisfaction questionnaire—simply check "Ms." You'll be making sure the issues that really matter to you (and most women) will also be taken more seriously by politicians and corporations.

Did You Know?

- Where voters can register using "Ms." (not all states offer "Ms." in their choice of titles), this address can be a more effective means than party labels for politicians to determine how many pro-choice female voters are out there.
- The more women who select "Ms.," the more likely politicians will be to note the large number of female pro-choice voters and enact pro-choice legislation.
- Politicians are increasingly taking note of the "Ms." contingency, ever since the 1991 Pennsylvania senatorial election in which unknown, pro-choice Harris Wofford unexpectedly defeated Dick Thornburg. As Bush's Attorney General, Thornburg had taken a vehement anti-choice stand.

- In a recent study, businesswomen using the title "Ms." were seen by professionals of both sexes as possessing the characteristics of a successful manager: "motivated, responsible, competent and in charge."

Five-Minute Solutions:

- If you're given the option on your voter's registration, register to vote using "Ms." It's a way of encouraging politicians, who may select "Ms." from the computers to identify how many pro-choice and pro-women's concerns constituents are out there, to develop more platforms and legislation to satisfy women voters. Time it takes to check "Ms.": one second.
- Check "Ms." whenever you return a product questionnaire, or a corporate employee form (except on benefit forms, where you may be required to check "Mrs." if you want family medical coverage). If it isn't offered as a choice, write it in and then check it.
- Consider joining the National Women's Mailing List (cost: a $3.50 donation), the *first* national communications database connecting women who care about improving women's status and choices: NWML, Box 68, Jenner, CA 95450; (707) 632-5763. If you join the list, groups working on issues of concern to women will then be able to find you. If you write to them, NWML will send you a registration form first, so you can check only the issues/types of items on which you really want to receive information (political candidates, reproductive rights, AIDS, incest, child care, women's professional groups, films, videos, books, and so on). NWML now has 60,000 members. In comparison, the Moral Majority claims to have 10 million in *their* database network. Isn't it time we had our own network to help serve women's needs?

42.

Get Women on the Road to the White House

• • • • •

Twenty years ago, two of our U.S. senators were female, and today there are still only two. While the number of women in state legislatures has increased, women are still largely excluded from the *top* rungs of the political ladder—the Senate, the House of Representatives, and the White House, where the old boys' network reigns supreme. Yet if women aren't sitting in top political seats, will we ever be able to: stop a male-dominated government from overturning *Roe* v. *Wade?* Protect women like Anita Hill from sexual (and senatorial) harassment? Attain equal pay? Luckily, right now we stand before a golden opportunity to put women in power and hasten change: recent surveys show the nineties are a uniquely good time for women candidates.

Did You Know?

- Women account for only 16% of elected officials in the U.S.
- Congress has had 11,320 members over the years, yet only 134 have been women.
- Women make up 32% of the national legislature in Sweden; 34% in Norway—and a paltry 5% (of the Senate and House) in the U.S.A.
- Over the past decade, the number of women appointed to federal courts has been steadily decreasing: women made up 15.5% of appointments to the federal bench under Carter; under Bush: 9.9% (so far).
- If current rates hold steady, it will be another 64 years before women make up 50% of local legislatures.

- Studies show women are *less* likely to win elections than male candidates (in 1990, seven women ran for the Senate but only one won), and yet, once women get into office, they're *more* likely to stand up for women's concerns.

How to Make a Difference:

- Show extra support to women who do run for office by donating funds to a female candidate you feel you can get behind. Right now, women candidates stand poised to benefit from voters' increasing disillusionment with the old male guard: according to a new poll, in today's political climate (where voters are looking for candidates who have a strong commitment on domestic issues) a Democratic woman now has a whopping 15-point margin against a Republican man. There are other indicators, too, that this might just be the year women make a big splash in Washington: in the seven weeks following the confirmation of Supreme Court Justice Clarence Thomas, donations to "EMILY's List," a group that raises funds for Democratic women candidates, rose 52%. (To find out who your local candidates are and where they stand on the issues, see Section 40: Get Ready to Fight for *Roe* in Your Backyard, p. 101.)
- If you can possibly afford it, join EMILY's list (EMILY is an acronym for "Early Money Is Like Yeast"). EMILY's list is the nation's most powerful donor network and political resource for pro-choice Democratic women candidates. They carefully research female candidates before offering support, and also provide members who join their "list" with a quarterly newsletter which keeps you up to date on all the candidates' stands on various issues—so you can make the most informed decision possible when you get to the polls. Although it's not cheap ($100 donation plus an agreement to make two more gifts of $100 to recommended female candidates per election cycle), it's well worth it. Because if men won't protect women's right to choice, or our right to be protected from violence, or to have reasonable family and maternity leave, we'll have to elect women who *will*.
- If you know someone who loves to cook or barbecue (man or woman), give the gift of the apron (yes, an apron) or T-shirt which says: "Clean up Politics. Elect Women." Send a check ($10 plus shipping) payable to the National Women's Political Caucus, c/o Mary Stanley, 1361 N. Del Mar Avenue, Fresno, CA 93728. Or call with a credit card number: (209) 268-5756.

Resources:

EMILY's List (EMILY is an acronym for "Early Money Is Like Yeast"), 1112 16th Street, Suite 750, Washington, DC 20036; (202) 887-1957.

Women's Campaign Fund, 120 Maryland Ave. NE, Washington, DC 20002; (202) 544-4484.

43.

Flex Your Voting Muscle
• • • • •

As 52% of the population, women already have enormous power to influence political decisions. Not only do voting-age women outnumber men in this country by 9 million, but 68% of women are registered to vote (compared to 65% of men) and we vote *more* than men do. In 1988, 58% of women voted (54 million) compared to 56% of men (48 million). Isn't it time we showed the real power in numbers?

Did You Know?

- It's only due to the voting gender gap (meaning women are more likely than men to vote for candidates who support issues like the right to choice, health care, family leave, and education) that Democrats now control Congress.
- To wit: in the 1990 elections for the Senate, men voted Republican 53% to 45%, but women swung in the opposite direction, voting Democratic 53% to 45%.
- 51% of women say the Senate hearings on the confirmation of Clarence Thomas to the Supreme Court made them consider women's issues in the 1992 presidential election more than they otherwise would have done.
- If every woman of voting age in America sent the President a postcard expressing her political beliefs (whatever they might be), the White House would be buried under 1050 *tons* of mail.

110

How to Make a Difference:

- Aside from the obvious step of letting your voice be heard at the polls, what else can you do? Track your congressperson's voting record before you go to the polls. Here's how to get started: contact Mary Stanley, a member of the advisory board of the National Women's Political Caucus (NWPC, 1361 N. Del Mar, Fresno, CA 93728). She has phone numbers and rosters for the Democratic and Republican political headquarters in every state (or, if you have those numbers already, go ahead and call your party headquarters for information on the candidates). She can also: tell you whether the NWPC has regional chapters based in your area; get you a copy/or information from the NWPC's *Voting Record on Women's Issues of the U.S. Congress* (for your own copy, send $4.25); and alert you to newsletters available in your area for voters who are concerned about women's issues in particular (for instance, in California, *Women's Alert:* [714] 869-3857, California State Polytechnic, University of Pomona, Pomona, CA 91768, is an excellent resource). Stanley can also send you an excellent booklet for $5 called *How to Change the World: A Woman's Guide to Grassroots Lobbying.* Call her at (209) 268-5756.

- See the chart, "Actions Speak Louder than Words," on p. 114.

Resources:

National Women's Political Caucus, 1275 K Street NW, Suite 750, Washington, DC 20005; (202) 898-1100.

44.

Actions Speak Louder Than Words— Your Senators' Scorecard
●●●●●

As we all know, in every election year, politicians who once knew precisely how they felt about various issues suddenly become elusive. Is a senator for or against spending money for child care or family leave? Where exactly does he stand on abortion? By listening to their well-rehearsed positions on the nightly news, it's often impossible to tell. To take the hot wind out of politicians' sails and to find out where your senator really stands, just check the charts on the following pages.

On each chart, senators have been given 20 points for backing a recent amended version of Senate bill S.5, the Family and Medical Leave Act that President Bush vetoed; 20 points for voting pro-choice at least 75% of the time on about a dozen different abortion bills, and 10 points if they sometimes vote pro-choice and sometimes don't (fence-sitters on abortion rights are indicated with an NW for "needs work"). Senators have also been given 20 points for supporting Anita Hill and voting against Clarence Thomas; 20 points under "For Women's Issues," given for voting at least 70% of the time in favor of a variety of bills of crucial concern to women (the issues, selected by the National Women's Political Caucus, range from better wages for child-care providers to abortion and job discrimination); and 20 points for supporting the Mitchell Child Care Act (which authorized $1.75 billion in child care subsidies to parents and day-care providers). Senators were then given an overall "women's concerns" rating—from 0% (meaning that senator never supports women's concerns) to 100% for those senators who are always behind us. (Because abortion is also included in the "For Women's Issues" column, a woman's right to choose is weighted slightly higher than 20% under "Overall Rating.")

112

How to Make a Difference:

- If you're upset (or pleased) with how your legislator has voted, write him or her. Just address mail to the senator of your choice at U.S. Senate, Washington, DC 20510.
- To find out the voting record of your U.S. representatives—so you can also give them feedback and vote against those who vote against our rights (by writing them at U.S. House of Representatives, Washington, DC 20515)—write or call Catholics for a Free Choice, 1436 U Street NW, Washington, DC 20009; (202) 986-6093. They have a wonderful eight-page booklet called *Actions Speak Louder* ($2) that rates the entire 101st Congress on "human rights issues"—in other words, the issues that most matter to women. (You don't need to be Catholic to utilize this valuable resource. It's for all women, regardless of their religious affiliation.)
- Create a letter-writing kit. Keep 10 or 12 stamped postcards pre-addressed to various elected officials in a desk drawer. When you see a news story about an abortion or Family Leave bill pending in Congress, take two minutes to jot down your personal story and mail the card on your way to work or the grocery store. For the holidays, make up gift kits for your friends.
- For tips on how to go about phoning your senator or representative, see "Phone for Action" in Section 20: Tell One Congressperson How Violence Against Women Has Harmed You (p. 56).

Actions Speak Louder Than Words—Your Senators' Scorecard

Senator	For Family Leave	Pro-Choice	For Anita Hill	For Women's Issues	For Child Care	Overall Rating (%)
ALABAMA						
Howell Heflin (D)	NO	NO	YES	NO	YES	40
Richard Shelby (D)[1]	NO	NW	NO	YES	YES	50
ALASKA						
Ted Stevens (R)	YES	NW	NO	NO	NO	30
Frank Murkowski (R)[1]	YES	NO	NO	NO	NO	20
ARIZONA						
Dennis DeConcini (D)	YES	NO	NO	YES	NO	40
John McCain (R)[1]	YES	NO	NO	NO	NO	20
ARKANSAS						
Dale Bumpers (D)[1]	YES	YES	YES	YES	YES	100
David Pryor (D)	A	YES	YES	YES	YES	80
CALIFORNIA						
Alan Cranston (D)[2]	YES	YES	YES	YES	YES	100
John Seymour (R)[1]	NO	YES	NO	?	?	?
COLORADO						
Hank Brown (R)	NO	NW	NO	NO	NO[4]	10
Timothy Wirth (D)[2]	YES	YES	YES	YES	YES	100
CONNECTICUT						
Chris Dodd (D)[1]	YES	YES	YES	YES	YES	100
Joe Lieberman (D)	YES	YES	YES	YES	YES	100
DELAWARE						
William Roth (R)	YES	NO	NO	NO	NO	20
Joseph Biden (D)	YES	YES	YES	YES	YES	100
FLORIDA						
Bob Graham (D)[1]	YES	YES	YES	YES	YES	100
Connie Mack (R)	NO	NO	NO	NO	NO	0
GEORGIA						
Sam Nunn (D)	YES	YES	NO	YES	NO	60
Wyche Fowler (D)[1]	YES	YES	NO	YES	YES	80

Senator	For Family Leave	Pro-Choice	For Anita Hill	For Women's Issues	For Child Care	Overall Rating (%)
HAWAII						
Daniel Inouye (D)[1]	YES	YES	YES	YES	YES	100
Daniel Akaka (D)	YES	YES	YES	YES	YES[4]	100
IDAHO						
Larry Craig (R)	NO	NO	NO	NO	NO[4]	0
Steve Symms (R)[1]	NO	NO	NO	NO	NO	0
ILLINOIS						
Alan Dixon (D)[2]	YES	NW	NO	YES	YES	70
Paul Simon (D)	YES	YES	YES	YES	YES	100
INDIANA						
Richard Lugar (R)	NO	NO	NO	NO	NO	0
Daniel Coats (R)[1]	YES	NO	NO	NO	NO	20
IOWA						
Charles Grassley (R)[1]	NO	NO	NO	NO	NO	0
Tom Harkin (D)	A	YES	YES	YES	YES	80
KANSAS						
Robert Dole (R)[1]	NO	NO	NO	NO	NO	0
Nancy Kassebaum (R)	NO	NW	NO	NO	YES	30
KENTUCKY						
Wendell Ford (D)[1]	YES	NO	YES	NO	YES	60
Mitch McConnell (R)	NO	NO	NO	NO	NO	0
LOUISIANA						
J. Bennett Johnston (D)	YES	NO	NO	NO	YES	40
John Breaux (D)[1]	YES	NO	NO	NO	YES	40
MAINE						
William Cohen (R)	YES	YES	NO	YES	YES	80
George Mitchell (D)	YES	YES	YES	YES	YES	100
MARYLAND						
Paul Sarbanes (D)	YES	YES	YES	YES	YES	100
Barbara Mikulski (D)[1]	YES	YES	YES	YES	YES	100

Senator	For Family Leave	Pro-Choice	For Anita Hill	For Women's Issues	For Child Care	Overall Rating (%)
MASSACHUSETTS						
Ted Kennedy (D)	YES	YES	YES	YES	YES	100
John Kerry (D)	YES	YES	YES	YES	YES	100
MICHIGAN						
Carl Levin (D)	YES	YES	YES	YES	YES	100
Donald Riegle (D)	YES	YES	YES	YES	YES	100
MINNESOTA						
Paul Wellstone (D)	YES	YES	YES	?	?	?
David Durenberger (R)	YES	NO	NO	NO	NO	20
MISSISSIPPI						
Thad Cochran (R)	NO	NO	NO	NO	NO	0
Trent Lott (R)	NO	NO	NO	NO	NO	0
MISSOURI						
Kit Bond (R)[1]	YES	NO	NO	NO	NO	20
John Danforth (R)	YES	NO	NO	NO	NO	20
MONTANA						
Max Baucus (D)	YES	YES	YES	YES	YES	100
Conrad Burns (R)	NO	NO	NO	NO	NO	0
NEBRASKA						
James Exon (D)	YES	NO	NO	NO	YES	40
Bob Kerrey (D)	A	YES	YES	YES	YES	80
NEVADA						
Richard Bryan (D)	YES	YES	YES	YES	YES	100
Harry Reid (D)[1]	YES	NO	YES	NO	YES	60
NEW HAMPSHIRE						
Robert Smith (R)	NO	NO	NO	NO	NO[4]	0
Warren Rudman (R)[2]	NO	YES	NO	NO	NO	20
NEW JERSEY						
Bill Bradley (D)	YES	YES	YES	YES	YES	100
Frank Lautenberg (D)	YES	YES	YES	YES	YES	100

Senator	For Family Leave	Pro-Choice	For Anita Hill	For Women's Issues	For Child Care	Overall Rating (%)
NEW MEXICO						
Jeff Bingaman (D)	YES	YES	YES	YES	YES	100
Pete Domenici (R)	NO	NO	NO	NO	NO	0
NEW YORK						
Alfonse D'Amato (R)[1]	YES	NO	NO	NO	YES	40
Daniel Moynihan (D)	YES	YES	YES	YES	YES	100
NORTH CAROLINA						
Jesse Helms (R)	NO	NO	NO	NO	NO	0
Terry Sanford (D)[1]	YES	YES	YES	YES	YES	100
NORTH DAKOTA						
Quentin Burdick (D)	YES	YES	YES	YES	YES	100
Kent Conrad (D)[2]	YES	NO	YES	NO	YES	60
OHIO						
John Glenn (D)[1]	YES	YES	YES	YES	YES	100
Howard Metzenbaum (D)	YES	YES	YES	YES	YES	100
OKLAHOMA						
David Boren (D)	NO	NO	NO	NO	YES	20
Don Nickles (R)[1]	NO	NO	NO	NO	NO	0
OREGON						
Mark Hatfield (R)	YES	NW	NO	YES	YES	70
Bob Packwood (R)[1]	YES	YES	YES	YES	NO	80
PENNSYLVANIA						
Harris Wofford (D)	YES	YES	YES	?	?	?
Arlen Specter (R)[1]	YES	YES	NO	YES	YES	30[3]
RHODE ISLAND						
John Chafee (R)	YES	YES	NO	YES	YES	80
Claiborne Pell (D)	YES	YES	YES	YES	YES	100
SOUTH CAROLINA						
Ernest Hollings (D)[1]	NO	YES	NO	YES	YES	60
Strom Thurmond (R)	NO	NO	NO	NO	NO	0

Senator	For Family Leave	Pro-Choice	For Anita Hill	For Women's Issues	For Child Care	Overall Rating (%)
SOUTH DAKOTA						
Thomas Daschle (D)[1]	YES	YES	YES	YES	YES	100
Larry Pressler (R)	NO	NO	NO	NO	NO	0
TENNESSEE						
Albert Gore (D)	YES	YES	YES	YES	YES	100
Jim Sasser (D)	YES	YES	YES	YES	YES	100
TEXAS						
Lloyd Bentsen (D)	YES	YES	YES	YES	YES	100
Phil Gramm (R)	NO	NO	NO	NO	NO	0
UTAH						
Jake Garn (R)[2]	NO	NO	NO	NO	NO	0
Orrin Hatch (R)	NO	NO	NO	NO	YES	20
VERMONT						
James Jeffords (R)	YES	YES	YES	YES	YES	100
Patrick Leahy (D)[1]	YES	YES	YES	YES	YES	100
VIRGINIA						
Charles Robb (D)	YES	YES	NO	YES	YES	80
John Warner (R)	NO	NO	NO	NO	NO	0
WASHINGTON						
Brock Adams (D)[2]	YES	YES	YES	YES	YES	100
Slade Gorton (R)	NO	NO	NO	NO	NO	0
WEST VIRGINIA						
Robert Byrd (D)	YES	NW	YES	YES	YES	90
Jay Rockefeller (D)	YES	YES	YES	YES	YES	100
WISCONSIN						
Robert Kasten (R)[1]	NO	NO	NO	NO	NO	0
Herbert Kohl (D)	YES	YES	YES	YES	YES	100

Senator	For Family Leave	Pro-Choice	For Anita Hill	For Women's Issues	For Child Care	Overall Rating (%)
WYOMING						
Alan Simpson (R)	NO	NO	NO	NO	NO	0
Malcolm Wallop (R)	NO	NO	NO	NO	NO	0

?   These newcomers weren't yet in the Senate when these issues were voted on. Their final rating should be considered with this in mind.

A   Did not vote or otherwise make a position known.

1   Up for reelection in 1992.

2   Either retiring or defeated in a primary.

3   Fifty percentage points have been subtracted for his harsh treatment of Anita Hill.

4   These legislators were members of the House of Representatives at the time the Mitchell Child Care bill was voted on in the Senate, so their child-care rating is based on their overall voting records on child-care while they were in the House.

NW   Needs work. Fencesitters on abortion rights, these senators score high on some pro-choice polls, less well on others. Good people to target when an abortion bill is coming up.

Chart based on data in *CQ Almanac; Conscience* magazine's July/August 1991 "Actions Speak Louder" supplement on the voting record of the 101st Congress; the *AAUW Voting Record, 101st Congress;* the National Abortion Rights Action League's "Congressional Record on Abortion 1990"; and the National Women's Political Caucus "Voting Record on Women's Issues, 101st Congress."

45.

Let the President Know
● ● ● ● ●

> In 1988, the White House sent an amicus brief
> (a "friend of the court" memo) to the Supreme
> Court which reiterated the White House posi-
> tion that "*Roe* v. *Wade* is so far flawed . . . that
> this Court should reconsider that decision and
> on reconsideration abandon it."—Briefs for the
> United States as Amicus Curiae in *Webster* v. *Repro-*
> *ductive Health Services* (1988) *and Thornburgh* v.
> *American College of Obstetricians and Gynecolo-*
> *gists* (1984).

It's no secret that George Bush has taken a firm stand against a woman's right
to choose an abortion (though political analysts say he may become temporarily
"fuzzy" about his anti-choice views right before the election in order to keep
women's votes). He has also twice vetoed the Family and Medical Leave Act, the
only piece of pro-family legislation to pass both houses of Congress.

One might wonder: is the message to women that you *should* have the baby,
regardless of your circumstances, but once you have the child there will be no
help from the government?

Regardless of how you feel about George Bush's ability to govern—and
whether you're a Republican or a Democrat—if you're disturbed by either of
these stands that our President has taken, Let the President Know. Here's how:

1. Call the White House comments line at (202) 456-1111 (this line
is *often* busy, so you may want to write instead).

2. Write in your thoughts and send in the postcard below. (And if another presidential candidate is elected in November, jot down your thoughts all the same, so he doesn't in any way soften his pro-choice stance once elected.

Pre-addressed postcard printed on the front with the words:
"Let The President Know" appears here.
Address on back:
The President
The White House
1600 Pennsylvania Avenue
Washington, DC 20500

IF YOU HAVE
MORE TIME

• • • • •

46.

Show Sexism Won't Sell
• • • • •

If you think you're seeing more and more subtly sexist messages in print and TV ads these days, you're not imagining it. In everything from beer ads to advertisements for women's fashion, advertisers—who used to be much more worried about not offending women—seem to have thrown all caution to the wind. They seem to think we don't care about how we're portrayed anymore. What can you do about this disturbing trend? As a consumer, you have buying veto power. Use your purchases to tell advertisers that sexist ads are *not* okay with you.

Did You Know?

- Advertising is a $41 billion-a-year industry.
- The biggest offenders of sexist ads? Beer and liquor advertisers (who've given us such scenarios as Old Milwaukee's "Swedish Bikini Team" and the Coor's Light message to women, "If you don't watch your figure, who *will?*").
- Ad agencies—run mostly by men—have few rules or procedures for spotting sexism in ads, and the National Advertising Review Board hasn't issued guidelines on the use of women in ads since 1978.
- By the time a young woman graduates from high school, she will have been bombarded by up to 350,000 commercials.
- Each one of us is exposed to between 300 and 500 ads a day.
- Although advertisers and networks say "sex sells," that's not necessarily the case, says one report, which found that nudes in ads do not enhance brand recall as much as "ads with forests and mountains do."

What You Can Do:

- Complain to the company—and go straight to the top. For $7.95 in any bookstore (or free at your local library) you can get *The World Almanac and Book of Facts,* which lists addresses and the names of CEOs for the top consumer companies in America. When you see an offensive ad, look up the manufacturer's address and dash off a postcard—to the *CEO* of the company (CEOs sometimes listen better than marketing directors do).

- Or, simply look on the packaging label of the product (for instance, the beer label, the clothing tags, etc.); there, you'll find the company's location and perhaps even their phone number. If not, information in the state where the company is located can give you their number and address. Call the company to get the CEO's name, and *write*. This should take you five minutes, tops.

- Leave 99 million bottles of beer (or liquor) on the shelves by buying less of those brands with offensive ads (or don't buy those brands at all). Consumer experts project women will spend $30 billion on alcohol by the year 1994. So if you're one of the 33 or more million women in this country who drinks beer occasionally, use your buying veto power. The next time you see a beer company use a flock of half-clad females to sell their brew, simply buy three less beers by that manufacturer this year. If all women who occasionally drink beer did so, we'd get that company's attention—or at least the 99 million bottles still sitting on their warehouse shelves would.

- When you see a sexist ad on television, call and let that network *know* you object to ads showing women in a negative, offensive light. Call the main headquarters for the network (ABC: [212] 456-7777; CBS: [212] 975-4321; NBC: [212] 664-4444; and FOX: [310] 277-2211) and ask for the Office of Broadcast Standards and Practices. Tell them the name of the product being advertised, and voice your objection to the ad. Networks have been known to pull commercials if they suspect continuing to run the ad will lose them loyal viewers.

Resources:

Media Watch, P.O. Box 618, Santa Cruz, CA 95061-0618, (408) 423-6355, has pre-addressed, pre-written postcards to help you get to the appropriate executives, advertisers, and marketers who are the worst offenders of sexism in advertising today. Call or write to subscribe to their quarterly newsletter (postcards are included). Subscriptions cost $15 to $20 a year.

If you want to get the scoop on how bad sexism in advertising really is, the widely acclaimed film *Still Killing Us Softly: Advertising's Image of Women,* which has been shown worldwide, is now available in video for rental through Cambridge Documentary Films, P.O. Box 385, Cambridge, MA 02139; (617) 354-3677. The rental cost of $46 plus $8 shipping is quite high, so you might want to rent it with a few friends. Or, ask your local library to purchase a copy and keep it on hand.

Child Care

47.

Have a Delinquent Dad's Taxes Withheld

• • • • •

One study found that divorced men are more likely to meet their car payments than their child support obligations. If your ex isn't paying what the courts ordered him to, use the new state and federal government "tax-intercept" program, through which the IRS withholds tax refunds from fathers who don't meet child support commitments. In 1990, 800,000 people used this program to collect $509 million for their children. You can, too.

Did You Know?

- $19 billion of child support is owed by fathers in the U.S.
- Nearly 10 million women raise children on their own today, up from 7 million a decade ago.
- Only 43% of women whose husbands now live in different states receive child support regularly (20% of dads move out of state after they've been issued a court order for child support).
- One quarter of the 5 million women who are supposed to receive child support get nothing, and another one quarter get only partial payments.
- In the last decade, the number of single mothers in the U.S. living below the poverty line increased by more than one third.
- If all the child support due single mothers was paid in full, it would be enough to pay the child care expenses for over 6 million children for a solid year.

What You Can Do:

- To find out how to get your ex's tax refunds withheld, contact your local child support agency to find out if you might be eligible, as well as how to apply. Get the phone number of your state's child support agency by calling the Child Support Project at The Children's Foundation: (202) 347-3300, or write to them (see Resources). If you write, request their list of Child Support Enforcement Offices, which costs $1 and lists the offices and grass-roots advocacy groups near you. Be sure to specify which state you live in. Or, call the Federal Office of Child Support Enforcement at the National Department of Health and Human Services Administration for Children and Families: (202) 401-9373. Also ask about wage withholding.

- Send a note to your congressperson or Senator supporting "The Child Support Recovery Act of 1992" (H.R. 1241, S. 1002) which would make it a federal offense for parents who owe child support to cross state lines in order to avoid making payments.

- If efforts through state child support agencies fail, consider contracting a private (rather than publicly funded, state-run) child support collections agency. For instance, Children Support Services in Maryland (see Resources) helps moms collect child support with the motto: "Kids need love *and* child support." Although they're a for-profit private company, their fees are on a sliding scale, based on the financial straits of the mother and child. They also do some pro bono work—and at most take only 25% of the money they recover from delinquent dads. But then, 75% for you is better than 100% of nothing. (If they can't help you, they may be able to refer you to other private agencies in your area that can.)

- To find out whether you're eligible for a new program, which allows some single moms to have dads who don't pay child support listed as credit risks with national credit-rating bureaus (information that won't be erased until your ex has paid up in full), contact the National Child Support Advocacy Coalition (NCSAC) at (703) 799-5659; P.O. Box 420, Hendersonville, TN 37077.

Resources:

The Children's Foundation, 725 15th Street NW, Suite 505, Washington, DC 20005-2109; (202) 347-3300. A good clearinghouse for women looking for referrals for child support agencies in their state, as well as information about wage withholding and placing liens against delinquent dads. They have several inexpensive bulletins and fact sheets on child support enforcement, such as "Child Support: An Overview of the Child Support Enforcement Problem" ($1), and "Child Support: Locating an Absent Parent via State and Federal Resources" ($1.25).

Office of Child Support Enforcement, Department of Health and Human Services Administration for Children and Families, 370 L'Enfant Plaza, Promenade SW, Washington, DC 20447; (202) 401-9373.

Children Support Services, 9811 Mallard Drive, Laurel, MD 20708; (301) 470-4294.

Get the free booklet *Handbook on Child Support Enforcement* by writing to Department 509Y, Consumer Information Center, Pueblo, CO 81009, for a quick overview of how the child support system works.

Association for Children for Enforcement of Support, Inc. (ACES), 723 Phillips Avenue, Suite J, Toledo, OH 43612, has a 24-hour hotline at 1-800-537-7072, or, between the hours of 8:00 A.M. and 5:00 P.M. ET, call (419) 476-2511. They can provide you with updates on current legislation affecting child support enforcement, and help you to understand your legal rights when it comes to establishing and enforcing child support payments.

48.

Invest in Woman-Friendly Companies

• • • • •

When investing, of course, your first priority is to protect your investment and get a good return on your money. Fortunately, you can do this *and* make the world a better place for women in one fell swoop. Next time you hear another dismal figure about how few women are promoted to upper management (example: the boards of directors at Fortune 500 companies are *still* 95.5% male), let your money speak your mind.

Did You Know?

- A poll of 400 senior executives in top American corporations found that when it comes to promoting women and minorities to senior positions, only 30% of executives report *their* company does a good job.
- Even when women do become managers, a "glass wall" keeps us in lower-paying areas such as PR and personnel.
- 60% of human resource managers say they don't feel comfortable putting women in "line jobs" (jobs that prepare them for top management).
- Yet these same managers say line-job experience is *essential* if an employee wants to get ahead.
- 99% of all secretaries, 93% of bookkeepers, and 82% of all clerks— but only 5% of our largest companies' CEOs—are women.

How to Make a Difference:

- Invest your hard-earned dollars in companies that are not only top-notch investments but *also* give women an equal shot at the brass ring. When you do, you'll be sending a message to the boardrooms of corporate U.S.A. that their future bottom line may depend on whether they open a door in their "glass wall" and a hatch in their "glass ceiling" for women to pass through. Since the 1980s, it's been possible to put your money into "socially responsible funds." These funds, which now handle $625 billion, carefully screen companies to find ones that are socially responsible yet profitable. Certainly, no matter where you put your money, you need to be careful—and only invest in funds you've thoroughly checked out. Here are some reputable woman-friendly funds you may want to look into (then judge them for yourself).

- Working Assets Money Fund (1 Harbor Place, Suite 225, Portsmouth, NH 03801; [603] 436-5152). This $240 million mutual fund invests only in companies with high financial yields *and* socially responsible policies (from promoting women and minorities to protecting the environment).

- The Social Investment Forum (430 First Ave. N, Suite 290, Minneapolis, MN 55401; [612] 333-8338). Marries social responsibility with shrewdness by selecting only funds with a one-year, proven track record. For $35 you'll get their quarterly newsletter; for a $65 membership fee you'll get the newsletter plus their directory of social investment services, which lists many woman-friendly financial advisers, funds, and services.

- One of the newest female-friendly mutual funds is WOMEN$HARE (launched January 1993). Here you can invest in "The Susan B. Anthony Fund," which puts your money only in companies that are excellent investments *and* address women's economic agendas. As a member you receive their bi-monthly newsletter, *The 52%*, which tells you which investments are good and why. An added plus: 10% of this fund's gross profits go to The WOMEN$HARE Foundation, which gives money to organizations addressing women's economic concerns. Contact Edith Conrad, 265 Charlotte Street, Apt. #10, Asheville, NC, 28801; (704) 259-9567.

- You can find out more about investing for a better world for women by getting *The Better World Investment Guide*, published by the

Council on Economic Priorities (1-800-729-4CEP; $19.95). This handy guide examines 100 of America's largest corporations and tells you exactly which ones offer women an equal shot at promotions and/or buy from women-owned firms when they purchase goods for their company. (American Express, Apple Computers, Digital Equipment Corp., Gannett Co., General Mills, IBM, and Kelloggs all come up big winners in one or both of these categories.)

One More Resource:

If you'd like to start investing but have no idea where to begin, you might want to check out WOMONEY: Financial Education and Counseling for Women (76 Townsend Rd., Belmont, MA 02178; [617] 489-3601). This financial planning service is set up to help you find investments that are socially responsible and female-friendly, while also meeting your personal investment goals.

49.
Find Out If Your Salary Is Equal
• • • • •

W hile women are making (very slow) progress on the job front, when it comes to equal pay for equal work, we have a long, long way left to go. Women who work full time make 74 cents to a man's dollar ($368 per week versus men's $497), which adds up to men pocketing *$6708 a year* more than women do for equal toil. If you wonder whether your salary is less than it would be if you were a man sitting at the same desk, first find out whether your salary is equitable with the five easy steps listed below. You might just want to share your findings with your manager or boss next time salary review rolls around.

Did You Know?

- Women managers in finance make even less compared to men— taking home less than 59% of what male financial managers earn.
- Women in health-diagnosing occupations (dentists, veterinarians, doctors, optometrists) make only 61% of what men in those jobs make.
- 93% of registered nurses are female, but male RNs make 10.4% *more*.
- Women in sales jobs earn 59 cents to a sales*man's* $1.
- Nearly three-quarters of women workers make less than $20,000 a year, while less than half of male workers do.

What You Can Do:

● Negotiating equal pay is a big step for every woman, and the proper approach differs according to each woman's work situation. But the first move is to educate yourself about pay discrepancies between men and women in your field. While wage discrimination is illegal and has been since the 1963 Equal Pay Act and the 1964 Civil Rights Act, Title VII, pay inequities continue to persist in the workplace—particularly in private corporations, which, unlike unionized occupations and the public sector (e.g., government workers), don't have to make salary policies public. If you work for a private company, how do you figure out whether you're being paid a fair wage compared to the men in your office in the same-level jobs? Here's a five-step plan:

1. Check industry trade publications at your local library. They frequently do salary surveys. For instance, *Adweek* does an annual salary survey for the advertising industry; Robert Half and Accountemps puts out an annual *Salary Guide* for those in finance, accounting and banking, and so on. Also consult *Working Woman*'s annual (January) salary survey, which provides "the information you need to get the money that will make you happy." Their 1992 salary survey covers 19 careers. (Or call *Working Woman* at [212] 551-9765 or [212] 551-9500 to order back issues.)

2. If you can't find the salary information you need through industry publications, contact the National Committee on Pay Equity (NCPE, see below). They'll give you information on men's vs. women's weekly earnings according to occupation (from the Bureau of Labor Statistics), as well as alert you to professional organizations in your field that will be able to help you even further.

3. Be aware when looking at salary surveys, however, that if you're in a profession which is predominantly female, you'll need to find a report that distinguishes male workers from female workers. Why? If you don't, you may be getting a skewed *low* average, since women's salaries (which are usually lower than men's even within predominantly female industries), will be overrepresented.

4. Find out about negotiating strategies by contacting NCPE. They can give you detailed, helpful tips on how women can negotiate fairer, better salaries.

5. Now, compile the information you have and refer to this information next time you come up for salary review, or when you're negotiating a salary for a new job. For instance, one high school counselor who heard about an opening for a corporate job researched what similar positions were paying ($28,000 to $35,000). Since her school salary was a measly $15,000, she worried that even if she was offered the job, she wouldn't be able to convince the company she deserved $13,000 to $20,000 more than she was making. When the three male interviewers offered her the position at a salary of $21,000, she looked down at her sheet of salary ranges, and replied sweetly: "Gentlemen, am I hearing you correctly? Is that a six-month's salary?" She got the job—and $32,500.

6. When you go into your next salary review or negotiation, ask for what you deserve. Until women get what we're worth, we'll never have real economic power, and economic power is the *key* to having equal say in all aspects of our lives.

Resources:

National Committee on Pay Equity (NCPE), 1126 16th Street NW, Suite 411, Washington, DC 20036; (202) 331-7343. Provides an information sheet on pay equity, a tip sheet on effective salary negotiation, and closely monitors local, state, and national pay equity activities. Get their bi-annual newsletter, *Newsnotes* (included in cost of membership, $35 or $15 for low-income members).

Violence Against Women

50.
Hang a Shirt on the Clothesline
• • • • •

I f you've ever been the victim of rape, incest, or child abuse—or if you've ever been battered—you can help create greater awareness about the need to combat today's widespread violence against women (as well as take a step toward self-healing) by creating your own "personal message" or decorated shirt for The Clothesline Project.

Did You Know?

- Of the nearly 4500 women murdered in the U.S. in 1989, almost 30% were slain by angry husbands or boyfriends. Only 5% of male victims were murdered by wives or girlfriends.
- One fifth to one half of American women were sexually abused as children, most by an older male relative.
- Girls are four times more likely to suffer childhood sexual abuse than boys.
- Girls are also significantly more likely to be the victims of physical abuse in their homes than boys are.

How to Make a Difference:

- If you have ever been the victim of one of these crimes against women, design and send a shirt, T-shirt, or blouse to The Clothesline Project. Similar to the AIDS quilt project, and sponsored by the Cape Cod Women's Agenda (see Resources) as part of their campaign to end the so-called war against women, this group encourages women to paint, sew, or embroider shirts which reflect their personal sorrow, outrage, fear, pain, and suffering. If you have a close female relative or friend who died as a result of one of these crimes, you might want to make a shirt in her memory. You might even use one of her shirts. Already displayed in twenty-six cities nationwide, from Boston to California, victims' shirts hang in outdoor public spaces (yes, fluttering on a clothesline) and draw attention to the number of American women who are assaulted, raped, and murdered every day.

- If you have more time, contact the Cape Cod Women's Agenda about bringing an exhibition of The Clothesline Project to *your* local area.

Resources:

The Clothesline Project, Cape Cod Women's Agenda, P.O. Box 822, Brewster, MA 02631; (508) 896-7530 or (508) 385-5443. Please write (rather than call) for more information before submitting a shirt, as different-colored shirts are used to represent victims of different crimes.

51.
Give Your Old Clothes to a Battered Women's Shelter
• • • • •

W e've all heard the bleak statistics on battering—every 15 seconds in the U.S. a woman is beaten by a man; 10 women are killed by their batterers every day. But in a few quick minutes, we can help those women who race into the night looking for refuge: next time you clean your closets or attic, set aside old clothes, sheets, toys, dishes, and anything else a battered woman and her children could use. Call the number for your state (see below) to locate the shelter nearest you. Then drop everything off when you're headed that way.

Did You Know?

- In 1987, approximately 375,000 women and children sought refuge in some 1200 shelters and safe homes across the country.
- 25% of abused women are battered during pregnancy (meaning many shelters need such items as maternity clothes, diapers, and baby powder).
- Though 3000 American women die every year from being battered and four million more are injured, many congressmen continue to call domestic violence a non-issue.
- The U.S. has four times as many shelters for abused dogs and cats as it does for abused women.
- In one Minnesota study, nearly 40% of women seeking immediate shelter were turned away for lack of space.

What You Can Do:

- If you already know how to find a shelter in your area, ask if they publish a "needs list" (many of the larger ones do). Examples: House of Ruth, 501 H Street NE, Washington, DC 20002 (202) 547-6173 (24-hour abuse hotline, 202-347-2777), regularly puts out a needs list, calling for such items as alarm clocks, toiletries (from toothpaste to sanitary napkins), mops, lamps, and canned food. Project Safehouse at the Center for Women's Studies and Services, 2467 E Street, San Diego, CA 92102, (619) 233-8984, has a "wish list" of similar items.
- If you don't know where to find a shelter, call the number below for your state. Battered women's shelters by their very nature have to be underground (so a batterer can't easily track down his victim). Thus, the most time-consuming part of all this may be locating a safe dropoff point for your donations.

  IMPORTANT: The following numbers are not crisis lines, but the numbers for administrative offices of state battered women's coalitions across the country. Because these offices often operate on shoestring budgets and are staffed by volunteers, you may have to leave your name and have someone call you back. Once you find out where to drop off donations, however, you can then do it regularly—whenever you have items a battered woman might need.

State coalitions:

Alabama: (205) 832-4842
Alaska: (907) 586-3650
Arizona: (602) 495-5429
Arkansas: (501) 793-8111
California (Central): (209) 575-7037
California (Northern): (415) 457-2464
California (Southern): (213) 655-6098
Colorado: (303) 573-9018
Connecticut: (203) 524-5890
Delaware: (302) 762-6110
District of Columbia: (202) 662-9666
Florida: (407) 425-8648

Georgia: (404) 524-3847
Hawaii: (808) 538-7216
Idaho: (208) 265-4535
Illinois: (217) 789-2830
Indiana: (812) 882-7900
Iowa: (515) 281-7284
Kansas: (316) 232-2757
Kentucky: (502) 875-4132
Louisiana: (504) 523-3755
Maine: (207) 324-1957
Maryland: (301) 974-2603
Massachusetts: (617) 426-8492
Michigan: (313) 954-1180
Minnesota: (612) 646-6177
Mississippi: (601) 435-1968
Missouri: (314) 634-4161
Montana: (406) 586-7689

Nebraska: (402) 476-6256
Nevada: (702) 358-1171
New Hampshire: (603) 224-8893
New Jersey: (609) 584-8107
New Mexico: (505) 526-2819
New York: (518) 432-4864
North Carolina: (919) 490-1467
North Dakota: (701) 255-6240
Ohio: (614) 221-1255 or (614) 382-8988
Oklahoma: (405) 360-7125
Oregon: (503) 239-4486 or (503) 239-4487
Pennsylvania: (717) 234-7353

Rhode Island: (401) 723-3051
South Carolina: (803) 232-2434
South Dakota: (605) 256-4319
Tennessee: (615) 242-8288
Texas: (512) 794-1133
Utah: No state coalition
Vermont: (802) 223-1302
Virginia: (804) 780-3505
Washington: (206) 484-7191
West Virginia: (304) 765-2250
Wisconsin: (608) 255-0539
Wyoming: (no number available when we went to press)

Resources:

If you have trouble reaching any of the above numbers, contact: The National Coalition Against Domestic Violence, P.O. Box 18749, Denver, CO 80218-0749; (303) 839-1852. They also have a nationwide directory of battered women's shelters and hotlines ($25), which gives a breakdown of the kinds of services provided, languages spoken, etc.

52.
Empower Yourself with Model Mugging
• • • • •

Graduates of personal-safety classes are often less likely to be raped, if attacked, than other women are. Of the hundreds of women in one Model Mugging self-defense program studied by Stanford University, 40 were later sexually assaulted, but 38 *escaped*—30 by stunning and disabling their assailants, 8 by frightening the men off. (The two women who were raped didn't fight back because their attackers were armed.) Consider taking a self-defense course to help prevent rape from happening to you, or to help protect yourself if you're ever attacked. (Also: experts say the physical and mental training provided by many personal-safety courses can give you a greater sense of power and confidence in all areas of your life—and projecting self-confidence and strength can lessen the chances that you'll ever be *selected* by an attacker.)

Did You Know?

- In 70% of rapes, the assailant is unarmed.
- Of those victims of sexual assault who fought back when attacked, 63% said their resistance helped protect them. Only 7% said it worsened the situation.
- Women who have self-defense skills—even if they choose to submit—recover 50% faster from the trauma of being attacked than other victims do.
- If every woman in America signed up for a self-defense course and used what she learned to defend herself against unarmed would-be

rapists, we might reduce the rate of completed rapes in the U.S. by as much as 70%.

How to Make a Difference:

- Sign up for a course like Model Mugging, started by men trained in martial arts who were fed up with watching women live in the shadow of male violence. Their goals? To teach women how to knock an unarmed assailant unconscious; how to fight while on the ground (where 90% of women quickly end up in a real assault); and how to defend yourself even when you feel so overwhelmed by fear you think you can't move or yell.
- Get Powerflex USA's self-defense training video, available fall 1992, which educates women about how to use intuition and prevention techniques to help *avoid* assault. The techniques have been created and are demonstrated by Al Marrewa (who's served as a rape consultant specialist for female employees at Time Warner and HBO). Call (310) 475-2772, or write Al Marrewa, MPH, Powerflex USA, Inc., 1015 Gayley Avenue, Suite 191, Los Angeles, CA 90024. (Cost of video isn't set yet.)
- If you're a runner, walker, or hiker, yet fear going out alone because of the possibility of assault, look into Project Safe Run. Started by a woman who was attacked by four men when she came home from work one day, this nonprofit organization lends women trained dogs to run or walk with them. Unlimited runs at any hour with a rigorously trained dog (who defends you only if someone shows aggression toward you) cost $25 a month (that's less than it would cost to feed your own dog for 30 days). Call (503) 345-8086 to see if there's a chapter near you, or write Project Safe Run, P.O. Box 22234, Eugene, OR 97402.

Resources:

Model Mugging has 18 branches from New York to California—call 1-800-443-KICK to be referred nationwide. It's expensive ($475 to $750 for five intensive sessions totaling 25 hours). If you can't afford that, don't despair. First, some Model Mugging branches offer financial assistance; and second, if yours doesn't, many local police departments, YMCA/YWCAs, martial arts studios, and health clubs also offer excellent, low-cost self-defense classes. Check the Yellow Pages for one in your area.

Chimera offers courses in seven states (GA, IL, OH, MA, NJ, SD, WI) that teach women, in an all-female environment, how to avoid and prevent assault. A six-week class costs $60. Call (312) 939-5341, or write 59 E. Van Buren, Suite 714, Chicago, IL 60605.

Women's Health Issues

53.
Clip for the Cure
• • • • •

At a time when breast cancer is killing American women at the record-breaking rate of 46,000 a year, research on this disease has never been more desperately needed. How can you help raise funds for this worthy cause if you have no time and less money? Simply get your hair trimmed on October 10.

Did You Know?

- During the 1990s alone, if no cure is found, half a million women will die of breast cancer—more than 10 times the number of men killed in battle during the Vietnam War.
- Half the women with breast cancer ultimately develop metastatic disease, for which the survival rate is only 18%—a figure that hasn't changed in 60 years.
- Breast cancer has taken nearly four times as many lives as AIDS since 1980. Yet in 1992 the federal government will spend 6 times more money on AIDS. While no one believes AIDS should get less money, activists suggest breast cancer has gotten the short shrift for so many years primarily because it's a "woman's disease."
- In 1991, angry breast cancer activists launched a letter-writing campaign that resulted in over 600,000 letters to Congress. Result: Congress ordered the National Institutes of Health to boost 1992 spending on breast cancer by 46%—to a total of $132.7 million.
- Despite this victory, the federal government will spend nearly thirty-three times less to fight breast cancer this year than it will spend on research and development for the Stealth (B-2) bomber.

What You Can Do:

- Do your part to boost research funding by getting a haircut for $10. Every year in October (Breast Cancer Awareness Month), the Regis Corporation sponsors a daylong "Cut-a-thon" at 1200 beauty salons nationwide and donates the proceeds to the Susan G. Komen Breast Cancer Foundation and the Canadian Breast Cancer Foundation to further breast cancer research. (The 1991 event raised about $300,000.) The 1992 Cut-a-thon will be October 10. To locate a salon near you, call 1-800-777-4444. Be sure to verify the time and location of the event, as some salons have so many clients on this day they have to move to larger quarters.

- If you can't bear to have anyone but your favorite stylist touch your hair, you can race for the cure, instead. Every year, in two dozen cities around the country, about 100,000 joggers pay a $10 to $15 entry fee to "Race for the Cure," with all proceeds going to breast cancer research. To see if and when a race will be held in your area, call the Komen Foundation at (214) 450-1777.

- Write legislators and the President, demanding more action not only on breast cancer but on all women's health issues.

Resources:

Y-ME, the National Organization for Breast Cancer Information and Support, Inc., 18220 Harwood Ave., Homewood, IL 60430, works to empower breast cancer patients, family, and friends, and is staffed by breast cancer patients. For information and support, call their hotline at 1-800-221-2141 (Mon.–Fri., 9:00 A.M. to 5:00 P.M., CT), or their 24-hour crisis line at (708) 799-8228. Their bimonthly newsletter *The Y-ME Hotline* (free with $15 membership) keeps you up on the latest research, clinical trials, and treatments.

A Final Word of Thanks
•••••

I'd like to extend my heartfelt thanks to the many experts, researchers, and organizations who shared their expertise during the creation of this book—it could not exist without them. While it is impossible to cite each study, researcher, and report that I drew upon in the space available to me here, it should be noted that I relied almost exclusively on primary sources when citing the hundreds of statistics that appear in this book.

My sincere thanks to those individuals who lent their help and offered up research, and/or whose research I drew upon, including: investigative reporter Russ Bellant; Mary Holland Benin and Debra A. Edwards, Arizona State University; Ida Bialik, National Association of Women's Yellow Pages; Suzanne Bianchi, Martin O'Connell and Arlene Saluter, U.S. Bureau of the Census; Susan Bishop, Bishop Associates; Conda Blackmon, Women in Communications, Inc.; Robert O. Bothwell, National Committee for Responsive Philanthropy; Linda Bursyn, American Civil Liberties Union Foundation in Los Angeles; Linda L. Carli, Ph.D., Wellesley College; Sofia Collier, Working Assets Money Fund; Ann Collins and Caroline Eichman, Child Care Action Campaign; Brenda Cooper, Ph.D., Trinity College of Vermont; Carolyn Edwards, Kennedy Publications; Eunice (Kitty) Ernst, National Association of Childbearing Centers; Susan Faludi, for her book *Backlash* (Crown: 1991); Rus Ervin Funk, Men's Anti-Rape Resource Center; Ellen Galinsky, The Families and Work Institute; Tracy Gary, Resourceful Women; Lynda Getchis, Security on Campus, Inc.; Katherine Gilday for her film *The Famine Within;* Carol Gilligan, the Harvard University Project on the Psychology of Women and the Development of Girls;

Frances Goldscheider and Linda J. Waite, *New Families, No Families?: The Transformation of the American Home* (University of California Press: 1991); C. Rose Harper, The Kleid Company, Inc.; Christopher L. Hayes, Ph.D., National Center for Women and Retirement Research; Joan Huwiler, NOW Legal Defense and Education Fund; Susan Horowitz, National Women's Mailing List; Kelly Jenkins, National Committee on Pay Equity; Kathie Kidder Jones, Urinette, Inc.; Joan Kanavich, Social Investment Forum; Jean Kilbourne, creator of the film *Still Killing Us Softly: Advertising's Image of Women*; Amy Langer, National Alliance of Breast Cancer Organizations; Janice Layman, *Marketing to Women*; David Lavalle, Senate Judiciary Committee; Lisa Lederer, Older Women's League; Claudia Lowe, National Association of Childbirth Assistants; Linda Meagher, International Association of Corporate & Professional Recruiters; Cathy Meredig, High Self-Esteem Toys Corp.; Carol Mollner, National Network of Women's Funds; Craig Norberg-Bohm, Ending Men's Violence Task Group; Barbara Otto, 9to5, the National Association of Working Women; Laura Phelps, Ward-Howell International, Inc.; Sara Pines, National Abortion Rights Action League; Maureen A. Pirog-Good and Jan E. Stets, editors of the book *Violence in Dating Relationships: Emerging Social Issues* (Praeger: 1989); Clarinda Raymond, Campus Violence Protection Center; Gerri Rosen, Women Helping Women; Peggy Reeves Sanday for her book *Fraternity Gang Rape: Sex, Brotherhood, and Privilege on Campus* (New York University Press: 1990); Virginia Sassaman and Jennifer Bills, Women's Legal Defense Fund; Anne Seymour, National Victim Center; Kathleen Shank, Montgomery Co., Pennsylvania, National Organization for Women; Tutti Sherlock, National Association of Child Care Resource & Referral Agencies; Jennifer Shein, Council on Economic Priorities; Ann Simonton, *Media Watch*; Denise Snyder, D.C. Rape Crisis Center; Mary Stanley, National Women's Political Caucus; Cassandra Thomas of the Houston Area Women's Center and the National Coalition Against Sexual Assault; Judy Lundstrom Thomas, *The Wichita Eagle*; Janet Tweed, Gilbert Tweed Associates; Glen Van Doren, Association of Executive Search Consultants; Robin Warschaw, for her book *I Never Called It Rape: The Ms. Report on Recognizing, Fighting and Surviving Date and Acquaintance Rape* (Harper & Row: 1988); Amy Wilkins, Children's Defense Fund; Joseph Weinberg, Joseph Weinberg & Associates; Naomi Wolf for her book *The Beauty Myth* (William Morrow: 1991); Leslie Wolfe, Center for Women Policy Studies; Toni Young, National Women's Health Network; and Esther Booth Zorn, International Cesarian Awareness Network.

My thanks, also, to the many additional organizations who lent their time and research, including: The Alan Guttmacher Institute; the American College of Surgeons Commission on Cancer—National Data Base; the American Association of Retired Persons; the American Association of University Women; the Bureau of Justice Statistics; the Bureau of Labor Statistics; Catalyst; the Center for Disease Control; Catholics for a Free Choice; the Feminist Majority Foundation; the Susan G. Komen Foundation; Korn Ferry International; LINK Resources; the National Association of Women Business Owners; the National Coalition on Television Violence; the National Commission on Working Women of Wider Opportunities for Women; the National Council on Alcoholism and Drug Dependence; the National Crime Survey; Regis Corporation; The Roper Organization; the U.S. Department of Commerce; the U.S. Department of Education, Office of Educational Research and Improvement; the U.S. Department of Health and Human Services; the U.S. Department of Justice, Uniform Crime Reports; Wellesley College Center for Research on Women; and the Women's Bureau at the U.S. Department of Labor.

I also drew upon research in many journals, including: *Alcoholism & Addiction; The American Economic Review; American J, Orthopsychiatric; American Journal of Public Health; American Journal of Sociology; Harvard Business Review; Journal of Advertising Research; Journal of American Medical Association; Journal of American Medical Women's Association; Journal of Family Issues; Journal of Marriage and the Family; Journal of the National Cancer Institute; Monthly Labor Review; The New England Journal of Medicine,* and *Obstetrics and Gynecology.*